Rescued from Satan

14 people recount their journey from demonic possession to liberation

Friar Benigno Palilla

Translated and commented by
Fr. Cliff Ermatinger

DEDICATION

To Father Matteo La Grua, on the anniversary of his death (January 15, 2012), my mentor in the exorcistic ministry, who, unbeknownst to me, suggested to Cardinal De Giorgio that I be named exorcist for the Archdiocese of Palermo so that his work would continue. For many years, he was a good Samaritan, caring for those afflicted by the Devil. I dedicate this book to him whose heavenly intercession has be instrumental in the deliverance of some people.

SPECIAL THANKS TO MICHELE AND CARRIE

Friar Benigno Palilla

Rescued from Satan

14 people recount their journey from demonic possession to liberation

Padre Pio Press

INDEX

Translator's Note and Forward to the English Version

It's easy to stay on the surface of things. It requires little thought and less will. Our common enemy finds great satisfaction in such slouching postures.

When dealing with a subject like demonic possession and exorcism, that same common enemy bristles a bit. He's happiest in the shadows. But since Hollywood has appropriated the subject with an endless of chain of burlesque representations, he'll settle for center stage if it's his own show: just so long as it's at the cost of putting Christ and a suffering member of His Mystical Body in the background. Of course, for such a movie, there has to be an exorcist. He's usually an odd guy: marginalized, anti-social, with a bag of tricks (and foibles) that make the audience question whether they'd rather fall into the hands of the Devil or this priest.

I knew Friar Benigno (or *Fra*, as the Italians would say) from a distance, sometimes hearing his conferences – always begun by singing a Latin hymn to Our Lady – at the International Association of Exorcists biennial meetings in Rome. One time, after I had given a conference to those priests, I repaired to the bar immediately afterwards to get a restorative dram. My single malt was soon interrupted by Fra Benigno's tapping me on the shoulder.

To put things into perspective, his diminutive stature is made up for his obvious gravitas, moral authority, and a face that reveals a man of profound prayer, asceticism, and strength.
"I don't agree with what you said in your talk. It doesn't apply to our situation in Italy".

"Not a problem for you or for me. My talk was descriptive, not prescriptive, so keep doing what you're doing", I said, perhaps a little too dismissively.

My mind went to work – not on what the unspoken disagreeable points might have been, but on something else. I had a little sabbatical time coming up, so this sounded like a good opportunity.

"As you know", I added, "there are no real experts in this field and I'm far from becoming one. What do you say if I spend a month with you to see how you work?"

"*Buona idea, la tua*", was his response. And that was that.

A year later I landed in Palermo. It was 52 degrees and everybody was wearing winter coats, many had hats, and some even had scarves. "These Italians", I thought to myself, "they don't know what cold is. I'm from the Midwest. Just a cassock is enough for me." Within 12 hours I was looking for street vendors to buy a hat, something I would never take off except in Mass or the shower. The humidity penetrates the bones like nowhere in the Midwest.

Upon arrival at Friar Benigno's friary, I was kindly received by all of the members of the community of *Frati Minori Rinnovati,* an austere Capuchin order. These are true sons of St. Francis: living in disused train cars converted into cells, they have no heating, no machines whatsoever, the food was extremely simple. Did I mention they had no heat?

After offering my Mass, praying a bit, and having lunch, Friar Benigno and I left for his work place. I observed him working with 6 or 7 cases of possession and oppression. When we were about to leave, his secretary said, "There's a boy here who started manifesting during the intake interview. Can you have a look at him?"

A 17-year old lad accompanied by very tired looking parents came in and sat down. He had a hard time answering the questions Friar Benigno put to him. His mother filled in the blanks, saying that the problems started when he began dating a girl involved in the occult two years before.

Friar Benigno began reciting the Litany of the Saints and the boy's eyes rotated in their sockets, becoming completely white. With the flick of a fingertip, he tossed the table that separated him from Friar Benigno and lunged at him. I tackled him, soon after his father joined in the attempt to subdue him. As we fought, symbols began to appear on his skin, pentagrams, crosses, all raised up like burn marks on his body. The boy shrieked with each new apparition. Meanwhile, Friar Benigno calmly prayed his prayers of exorcism

"Levate," ("Get off me' in Latin), the demon said to me calmly.

After an hour or so, my cassock was soaked through with sweat. When everything had calmed down, all I could think about was getting that knit hat. Palermo can get quite cold, I found.

Regarding remaining on the surface of things and first impressions, I ought to add that everything that was immediately apparent in Friar Benigno's face is true. But after living and working with him for a month, I must add that the fuller truth of this priest according to the Heart of Christ is a loving kindness, tenderness, and patience lived out in his human contacts those divine. He spends long hours before his Eucharistic Lord every day. Hence, the very apparent gravitas, strength, asceticism that are immediately apparent, and the divine charity that animates it all.

****

A year after that auspicious Sicilian welcome, I met Friar Benigno again in Rome. We spoke to each other about our most recent books and decided to swap titles: I would translate this book and someone at *Casa Editrice Amen* in Palermo would translate into Italian and publish *The Devil's Role in the Spiritual Life in the Writing of St. John of the Cross* (Padre Pio Press). It seemed like a good deal, for me, anyway.

So here we are.

Before proceeding with the original text, I thought it necessary to make some pointed commentary to put things in context. My intention with this brief commentary is not to write a treatise on possession and exorcism, but rather to provide some theological and experiential context for some of the things presented in the following pages.

I ought to preface this by saying that, in this field, there seem to be more unknowns than knowns. We are constantly learning. On the other hand, the Scriptures, Tradition, and the Church's collective experience over the last 2000 years provide us with some guiding principles.

As the reader will discover, much of the possessing demon's dialogue seems quite basic, if not to say banal. Sometimes we are presented with a dialogue that seems to come out of a B-movie - not that demons are incapable of high falootin' discourses (see Fabio's case). Their superior intellects can seem somewhat compromised by their twisted wills.

This shouldn't strike us as odd since we find a similar phenomenon in our own human experience. If we think of a culture that scoffs at the Middle Ages, an epoch that produced the most beautiful architecture, the greatest thinkers, and turns away from the Source of all truth, goodness, and beauty, we shouldn't be surprised at how ugly we moderns make things ourselves: modern art, hideous churches made that way in the name of functionality (yet fail to provide their most primordial function, that of giving worthy worship to God), and what need be said about the present state of academia? All of this ugliness reveals the spiritual and moral physiognomy of its producers.

To him who has been given much, much will be expected. Gifts come with responsibility. When an angel or a man made in the image and likeness of God falls, the fall is, indeed, very great. And the results are hideous.

Why does the Devil possess people?

Because it's ugly.

If foreknowledge of the Incarnation was cause of Satan's rebellion, Scripture alludes to this and Church Fathers confirm it, then each possession is a sort of mockery of the Word made Flesh. When God the Father looked lovingly on Christ, proclaiming Him His beloved Son on Mount Tabor, Satan's response is follow up that beautiful scene with the spectacle of a distraught father presenting his possessed son to inept disciples (Mt 17).

If one of the most sublime mysteries of the spiritual life is that of the divine indwelling, the Blessed Trinity making of the human soul its dwelling place (or "my heaven on earth", as Christ confided to St. Faustina), what a mockery of this reality when Satan or his minions come and make of the human body their dwelling place. On the other hand, it must be affirmed that some few saints have been possessed through an exceptional permission of Providence, casting no shadow on their sanctity or character, rather, in their cases, highlighting it. So it must be affirmed that in the merely moral realm, one venial sin, any offence against our Lord, is infinitely worse than a possession. Sin compromises our relationship with the Lord and is, therefore, Satan's greatest victory.

How can we know someone is possessed?
When there is an extraordinary encounter of a demon and a man in the form of a possession, there are some primary signs that confirm the situation:

- Knowledge of secrets (see Lorenzo's and Jerry's testimony);
- Knowledge or understanding of languages one has not learned (the young man already referred to in this section);
- Superhuman strength (ditto);
- Aversion to the sacred (take you pick from any testimony)

Although the last is the easiest to fake, and the penultimate sign can be questionable in some cases, the first two are the ones that bring the most certainty – especially when paired up with any of the other primary signs.

With regard to secondary signs, they are myriad. Nonetheless, after a while in this work (experience and consultation can be wonderful teachers), one discovers patterns and can proceed with more confidence.

"That which is received is received according to mode of recipient", so said Aristotle. He provides us with an important principle for this work, since the Devil, very capable of producing all sorts of primary and secondary signs, is happiest when in the shadows, working silently, secretly, for the condemnation of souls. Working on humans in what seem to be very human ways. Possession and oppression are certainly not his goal; rather, these are perks he allows himself. Since misery loves company, his real aim is that we end up where he is. Forever.

Often, his twisted will outdoes his intellect and he overplays his hand. The torments he couldn't resist heaping upon a possessed person who is concomitantly in a state of sin (not the same thing, and, as mentioned, certainly not of equal value!), can be precisely what leads the person to seek out an exorcist and, rather than find mere deliverance, discovers Christ. And in doing so, he returns to path that leads to salvation.

Among the secondary signs we find something similar to reading of minds, but there is a difference. In the case of Lorenzo or Jerry, we see that the possessing demon communicates to them what he knows through his own angelic nature. Although this supersedes human nature, it is in keeping with angelic nature. While angels and demons cannot read our thoughts, they do have a very good idea of what's going in our lives and heads, reading us quite well. Transmitting such information to the possessed person's mind can make him believe he reads minds.

Further, Thomas Aquinas agrees with St. Augustine that demons cannot produce miracles. On the other hand, what they can bring about can very well seem miraculous, just as it must seem somewhat miraculous to our pets that we can actually use a can opener to open up their food. Although it's far beyond their ken, it's all in a day's work for us. So too, for angels and demons. The devil cannot cure illnesses he didn't provoke. That would be a miracle. So, when we read Josie's testimony – one that stretches our imagination beyond any known zone of comfort – we are confronted with the disconcerting scenario of a stack of phenomena she wrought through agency of demons. The illnesses she "cured" were already the Devil's work. The Devil can imitate every symptom of illness – and take them away, so long as it's his (again, see Lorenzo). He can also mimic death – albeit briefly – as in the case of Josie.

If the Church provides us with such indicators, it also provides us with first principles for this work: faith (it keeps us obedient to the Church and subject to our Lord), prayer (it keeps us united to Him in a loving relationship), fasting (it keeps us humble, aware that whatever good is done is our Lord's work, and no one else can claim proprietor's rights).

****

I attempted to translate the text faithfully, taking into account some idiomatic phrases that simply don't work in English, but maintaining the original simplicity of expression. Some of these people are well educated, others not so much. While not trying to improve on the literary quality of the original text, or make them appear more erudite than, I did take it upon myself to edit out some superfluous repetitions.

Any failings or any lack of clarity belong to the translator.

INTRODUCTION

As the Bible and Church magisterium reveal – along with my own personal experience as an exorcist for the last 17 years – the Devil and his demons truly exist and today, just does as in the time of Jesus, continue to torment people with their ordinary activity (temptation), as well as their extraordinary activity, consisting of infestation, obsession, oppression, and possession.

Just as in the time of His earthly life, Jesus, in His mercy, cast out demons from possessed people; so too today, He continues to cast them out. Since *his mercy knows no bounds* (cfr. Lam 3:22), He continues to do so through the Church, to which He gave the power and the authority over demons with his precise command: *Cast out demons* (Mt 10:8).

What follows is an overview of this book's trajectory:

Part I.

First of all, we are presented with Jesus' exorcistic activity as found in *The Gospel of Mark*. Beyond the overwhelming evidence of the existence of the Devil and his demons through this activity, we are able to contemplate the merciful love of Jesus, revelation of the merciful love of God the Father. In his Bull of Indiction of the Extraordinary Jubilee Year of Mercy, Pope Francis writes in *Misericordiae Vultus*:

The mission Jesus received from the Father was that of revealing the mystery of divine love in its fullness. "God is love" (*1 Jn* 4:8,16), John affirms for the first and only time in all of Holy Scripture. This love has now been made visible and tangible in Jesus' entire life. His person is nothing but love, a love given gratuitously. The relationships he forms with the people who approach him manifest something entirely unique and unrepeatable. The signs he works, especially in favour of sinners, the poor, the marginalized, the sick, and the suffering, are all meant to teach mercy. Everything in him speaks of mercy. Nothing in him is devoid of compassion (*MV* 1).

Truly, Jesus is nothing other than love itself, a love that gives itself gratuitously; and the signs that He gives, including those in His dealings with the possessed by granting them deliverance, act as a hallmark of His mercy. Evidence of this is given after the deliverance of the Gerasene demoniac, to whom he entrusted this mission: *Go home to your family and announce to them all that the Lord in his pity has done for you* (Mk 5:19).

Everything in Jesus speaks of mercy and, seeing him, we can contemplate the mercy of Father: *Philip, whoever has seen me, has seen the Father* (Jn 14:9). The mercy that Jesus shows the Gerasene demoniac, as well as towards the other possessed people, delivering them, is precisely the mercy that God the Father has towards the possessed.

Part II

In the second part of the book, we find 14 testimonies. It recounts the stories of people who have been delivered by Jesus through the ministry of exorcism that has been entrusted by Him to the Church, Much like the Gerasene demoniac, they too have experienced the Lord's mercy.

Part III

In the third part of the book we delve into the theme of spiritual combat, given that, although the mercy of the Lord knows no bounds, it is equally true that diabolical activity is not over and continues to torment people. We are all called to battle.

Part IV

And lastly, I provide some pastoral suggestions corroborated by my own personal experience for the carrying out of the ministry of exorcism.

I would hope at this book is read by our bishops to help them understand the suffering to which the possessed person is subjected, thus, encouraging them to name at least one exorcist for their diocese, if they have not already done so. With this in mind, I would like to present the words of Cardinal De Giorgi:[1]

---

[1] Cardinal Salvatore De Giorgi, Address given at Regional Convention for Sicilian Exorcists, February 17, 2016.

Today more than ever the ministry of exorcism is among the most necessary and urgent for the Church in its missionary expanse to the existential, material, and above all, moral peripheries as the sacramental extension of Jesus, Doctor of souls and bodies, who has not ceased and will not cease to deliver the possessed.

If 'In this Holy Year,' as Pope Francis reminds us in his Bull of Indiction of the Extraordinary Jubilee Year of Mercy, 'we look forward to the experience of opening our hearts to those living on the outermost fringes of society: fringes which modern society itself creates, then how many uncertain and painful situations there are in the world today! How many are the wounds borne by the flesh of those who have no voice because their cry is muffled and drowned out...Let us open our eyes and see the misery of the world, the wounds of our brothers and sisters who are denied their dignity' (*MV* 15), you can no longer ignore the fact that among these situations of physical and spiritual suffering are found those of diabolical oppression, obsession, and possession, which make up the most dramatic suffering.

If, therefore – according to what the Pope tells us – "the Church is called to heal the wounds, applying the oil of consolation, binding them up with Mercy and healing them through solidarity and proper attention" without falling into "humiliating indifference" or "destructive cynicism", how much more then are we to "Open our eyes to see the wounds of so many of our brothers and sisters", who find themselves in precisely that sort of suffering", so that he will "hear their cry for help" (*MV* 15). If the spiritual works of mercy joined to the corporal works of mercy make up steps along the Jubilee pilgrimage, as recommended by the Pope, we find amongst them that of consoling be afflicted; that is, the ministry of exorcism and the most exalted work of consolation, because it is oriented towards the most physically and spiritually afflicted of all, those tormented by the devil.

At this point I think it important, to highlight the following indication offered by the Italian bishops in their presentation of the new ritual (No. 16): "The faithful who requests and exorcism is one of the members of the community who ought be shown preferential love: when subjugated by the power of the Evil One, he becomes the poorest of the poor, deserving our help, understanding, consolation. The exorcistic ministry, consequently, beyond a ministry of deliverance, is above all, a ministry of consolation." For sure, during a possession, the mystery of iniquity is at work in the world (cfr. 2 Thess 2:7) and, in a particular way clearly manifest (cfr. Eph 6:12): consequently, through the exorcistic ministry, the mystery of mercy must also be clearly manifest in I direct way, far above and beyond the powers of evil. Hence, above all during the Jubilee Year of Mercy, the need to promote the presence and passed from ministry of exorcism in every diocese of the world.

Yes, it is hoped that all the bishops, with mercy and a sense of urgency, promote the pastoral ministry of exorcism, naming at least one exorcist for their respective dioceses, if they have not already done so. Better still, beyond doing just that, from time to time – as I said in *Appendix* 1 of the book *La mia possession,* by Francesco Vaiasusso – "they ought to meet these poor christs and exorcise them, because, and I say this with confidence and all of the respect owed to the successors of the Apostles, it is not normal that a bishop should never have done an exorcism. That being the case, they cannot have practical knowledge of what it is and what it involves; just as it would not be normal for a bishop to never have given absolution, or to have celebrated ever a Holy Mass, all the while being put in charge over those who do these things. Saint John Paul II, in spite of his innumerable tasks, performed exorcisms – and he was the Pope!... How beautiful it would be if our bishops, at least sometimes, did what Jesus and the apostles did habitually."[2]

I would also hope that this book be read by medical specialists and, especially psychiatrists and those mental health professionals who maintain that all of the disturbances that people undergo can be reduced to psychological maladies. More particularly, I would be delighted if Federica Di Giacomo, director of the documentary *Deliver Us,* who has the honor (!) of showing us what exorcism is not and provides a wonderful lesson for new exorcists so they can learn what not to do. In her horrible interview with Antonella Gaeta, published in *la Repubblica,* September 2, 2016, upon being asked what is Evil, she responded:

---

[2] *La mia possessione,* ed. Piemme, Milano, 2012, p. 257.

A mental condition going to obsessive dependency. In the film (*Deliver Us*) possession is a metaphor for any dependence that one may have, such as drugs or dangerous games. Whoever plays with these things is possessed by something, Society continually produces this dependence, it becomes ever more difficult to maintain one's freedom and clarity. The Devil, therefore, becomes a conceptual receptacle where everything ends up. This is our universal history which always diminishes human responsibility.

With this response, the director totally dismisses the ministry of exorcism that the Church has provided for 2000 years by explicit mandate of Jesus Christ. Practically speaking, she says that the Devil does not exist, nor are diabolical possessions real, for that matter, because everything can be reduced to psychological problems.

Thus, even the cases narrated in this book, would be for Federica Di Giacomo, cases of persons afflicted with the psychological pathologies. Nonetheless, she ought to know those afflicted with such illnesses can only be healed by submitting them to medicinal treatment and psychotherapy. Without these two means, such a sick person could not achieve health. Yet the people in this book who tell their own story were all healed through exorcism, not by being submitted to medicinal treatment or psychotherapy.

And meanwhile, they have been healed. How do you explain that?

Certainly it is not a placebo effect, given that their healing was brought about, from beginning to end, through exorcism, carried out over the arc of several years. If this were the case of true placebo effect, it would have been taking care of in the first encounter with the exorcist, not the last.

The Church has an explanation in light of its power over all of the demons, that Jesus has given her, in that command received from Him to exorcise: *Cast out demons* (Mt 10:8). It is clear to the Church that the Devil and his demons do exist, as do demonic possessions, even as the Church warns the exorcist to not give immediate credence to everyone he confronts claiming to be possessed by a demon because it could very well be a case of illness, above all of a psychological nature or simply fruit of one's imagination (*Praenotandae* 14). The Church invites him to distinguish well between those cases of diabolical aggression from those that derive from a certain credulity (or "false opinion", as it says in the original Latin text), leading some people to consider themselves the object of a curse or a spell, bringing misfortune upon themselves, their families, and their possessions (*Praenotandae* 15).

With that, I do not mean that Federica Di Giacomo and unbelieving medical or psychiatric specialists ought to admit the existence of the devil and the possibility of possession. Such an affirmation is only possible if one has faith. Nonetheless, in their own intellectual honesty, they ought to admit that there are certain pathologies that escape their understanding, many of which disappear through the prayers of exorcism.

Such an admission could very well be the beginning of a healthy cooperation between medical professionals and exercise. On the one hand, exorcists could send some people who turn to them for help to medical and psychiatric professionals, whom they have determined to be affected by pathology, and not a spiritual problem of a demonic nature. And those same medical professionals and psychiatrists, could send people to the exorcists, who present an inexplicable symptomology that escapes their medical categories and continue to languish when submitted to their normal regimen of medicine and therapy. Such cooperation, far removed from personal interpretations and ideologies, would result in a great service to many suffering people.

Finally, by means of this book, I would like to awaken the readers to a sense of praise and thanksgiving towards the Lord. For my part, I must give testimony of it, having witnessed it in my exorcistic activity, and the ensuing deliverances and healings of many people. It has brought me to praise, bless, and give thanks to the Lord for having given the Church this power and authority over demons, even onto casting them out.

Part I

"ANNOUNCE TO EVERYONE WHAT THE LORD, IN HIS MERCY, HAS DONE FOR YOU" (Mk, 5:19)

The exorcisms of Jesus in The Gospel of Mark, Tangible manifestation of his mercy

Pope Francis wrote in his Bull of Indiction of the Extraordinary Jubilee of Mercy "*Misericordiae Vultus*:

> The mission Jesus received from the Father was that of revealing the mystery of divine love in its fullness. "God is love" (*1 Jn* 4:8,16), John affirms for the first and only time in all of Holy Scripture. This love has now been made visible and tangible in Jesus' entire life. His person is nothing but love, a love given gratuitously. The relationships he forms with the people who approach him manifest something entirely unique and unrepeatable. The signs he works, especially in favour of sinners, the poor, the marginalized, the sick, and the suffering, are all meant to teach mercy. Everything in him speaks of mercy. Nothing in him is devoid of compassion (*MV* 8).

If Jesus is the personification of love, giving up himself gratuitously, he was not so exclusive in his dealings with sinners and the indigent, excluding the sick and the suffering, as Pope Francis affirms, but also including in his ministry those possessed and vexed by demons. And his relations with them, as the Gospels show, something unique and irrefutable is revealed. The signs that marks His dealings with them bear the seal of mercy.

Having come to Peter's mother in law's house, it has grown late and they brought to Jesus all sorts of sick and possessed. He was not only merciful when dealing with one of these groups, neglecting the other. He did not only heal those who were afflicted with illnesses, but moreover, with his word alone (cfr Mt 8:16) cast out many demons (cfr Mk 9: 32-34).

When he healed the two blind men who followed him crying out: *Son of David, have pity on us*, they also brought to Jesus a man possessed by a mute demon. Here too, his mercy brought him beyond the healing of the two blind men, casting the demon out from that man, who was then able to speak (cfr Mt 9:32-33).

One day, while Jesus was teaching in the synagogue on the Sabbath day, it happened that they brought to him a woman who had been oppressed by a demon for 18 years, leaving her bent over, unable to stand up straight. Jesus looked at her and called her over, saying: *Woman, be freed of your infirmity*, and laid his hands upon her. Immediately she stood up straight, and glorifying God. But the synagogue leader, indignant because Jesus had carried out the healing on the Sabbath, turned to the crowd saying: *There are six days in which to work, on those days you should heal, not the Sabbath.* The Lord responded, *Hypocrites, doesn't each of you untie his donkey or mule on the Sabbath and bring him to drink? So should not this woman, a daughter of Abraham, whom Satan has kept bound for eighteen years, be set free on the Sabbath from what bound her?* (cfr Lk 13:10-17).

Here, we can contemplate the merciful heart of Jesus, which, with great tenderness, bends down to that woman, whom Satan had bounded up for 18 years, freeing her and restoring her to health: *She stood up straight and glorify God.*

For sure, if Jesus was merciful towards those people who were victims of extraordinary diabolical activity, it is owed to the fact that nothing in him lacked compassion and mercy, as Pope Francis rightly says. Let us reflect more closely on this aspect of His mercy and compassion towards the possessed, focusing on his exorcistic activity as found in the Gospel of Mark. To this end, I give the word to a Bible scholar, his Excellency, Bishop Giuseppe Costanzo, Bishop emeritus of Siracusa, who dealt with the subject in a masterful way during the Third Regional Conference of Sicilian Exorcists, that took place in the *Centro Maria Immacolata di Poggia*, in the Province of Palermo, February 8-10, 2007, when he was still Archbishop of Siracusa. The conference existed only in recorded form, so, in transcribing it, I broke it up into sections and sub-sections. I presented it to him for his review and, at the same time, asked permission to publish it, something he graciously granted.

GENERAL OBSERVATIONS IN THE GOSPEL OF MARK

The Gospel according to Mark, more then the other Gospels, deals with Jesus' mercy towards the possessed, offering four of the seven exorcism narratives we find in all of the Synoptics. It is to be noted (quite interesting, indeed!) that the first three of these four exorcisms are related to the first arrival of Jesus to a particular place:

- His first arrival to the synagogue in the Capharnaum (Chapter 1). There, in the cleanest and holiest of places, in the place where the Word of God is heard and prayed, Jesus discovers a demoniac and carries out an exorcism.

- Further, He distances himself from Israel, for the first time, enters the Decapolis, half pagan - half Jewish. There too, Jesus performs an exorcism on the Gerasene demoniac (Chapter 5).

- When he enters the completely pagan district of Tyre and Sidon, pagan city extraordinaire of the Phoenicians, Jesus also performs an exorcism (Chapter 7).

- Then, in Chapter 9, we find the deliverance of a possessed boy. While important in and of itself, it is also important in its ecclesiological and Christological vision.

Therefore, as is obvious, it is important to listen to Mark. Reading his Gospel gives us the impression that Jesus' Mission is a continual confrontation with Satan, whom He has come to destroy through His deliverance of man, held bound in his power. This is put in evidence not only in the exorcism narratives proper, but moreover through the numerous summarizing annotations scattered throughout various other contexts:

- After being vested with the Holy Spirit, Christ's first gesture is to confront Satan in the desert (Mk 1:12-13). He was "driven" (interesting verb usage) into the desert for this purpose.

- Note too, that his first public interaction ends up with a deliverance from an unclean spirit.

Mark's terminology is varied: Satan, unclean spirit, demon. For Mark, these terms are interchangeable. In Chapter 3:22-30, for example, he speaks in differently using the terms Satan, demon, unclean spirit. So much for terminology.

Mark deals with the figure of Satan, and presents him in his Gospel in diverse literary contexts:

- In the exorcism narratives;

- In various moments of the life of Jesus;

- In His controversies with the scribes;

- In reference to His own missionary activity;

- And in the missionary texts, in which the Apostles were sent out to preach and cast out demons.

At first glance, it provides us, if only provisionally, with the three emphases (in general terms).

First emphasis. In the confrontation with Satan three subjects are involved: Christ, man, the disciples. Satan is never dealt with alone. Mark is not in the least interested in Satan, since he merits know such attention. Satan is not dealt with in and of himself, but always in relation to Christ, in relation to man, and in relation to disciples. He speaks of Satan in order to:

- Reveal the meaning of Christ's mission;

- Reveal mans situation;

- Reveal the task of the Christian community.

Second emphasis. Satan is present in Jesus' Ministry and continues to be present throughout the history of the Church. This is important. Satan is already vanquished, and yet he continues to threaten man's existence.

Third emphasis. The spirit of evil is manifest in different forms and on the different levels: in temptations, an illness, in possession, in opposition to God's plan. In this chapter we proposed to verify these three emphases. So let's begin

FIRST EXORCISM: THE DEMONIAC IN THE SYNOGOGUE OF CAPHARNAUM

The text:

Then they came to Capernaum, and on the sabbath he entered the synagogue and taught. The people were astonished at his teaching, for he taught them as one having authority and not as the scribes. In their synagogue was a man with an unclean spirit; he cried out, "What have you to do with us Jesus of Nazareth? Have you come to destroy us? I know who you are - the Holy One of God!" Jesus rebuked him and said, "Quiet! Come out of him!" The unclean spirit convulsed him and with a loud cry came out of him. All were amazed and asked one another, "What is this? A new teaching with authority. He commands even the unclean spirits and they obey him.

As already mentioned, this is Jesus' first public intervention in the Gospel of Mark: the deliverance of a demoniac.

A possessed man in the synagogue begins to manifest during a liturgical service. Think about it: this is a moment of great density and intensity. At first everything is going well. The people are impressed and even marvel at Jesus' teaching, but within the synagogue, the very presence of Jesus reveals something that lay hidden. One of those present is a demoniac. This passage has a completely strategic position with regard to the entire Gospel of Mark. Precisely when Jesus is presented for the first time in a Jewish synagogue, his presence reveals something that ought to be removed. This is important from the strategic point of view and the message that Mark wants to provide.

Jesus silences is the unclean spirits, commanding him dryly: *Quiet, come out of him.* The spirit is obliged to obey; the liberated man comes back to himself.

Jesus' exorcism is radically different from those exorcisms practiced in Judaism and surrounding pagan – Hellenistic culture.

For example, there is no hint that Jesus used magical formulas similar to those of the pagans. Nor did Jesus' action find its efficacy in imploring God's help, or by using those exorcistic formulae familiar to the Jews.

Jesus cast out demons with the strength of His word and as a result, the demons submit. This is why the crowd marvels, because it understands that in Jesus, His word is peremptory, decisive, authoritative. This is the reason for their awe.

It is also important to note the difference between how Jesus confronts illnesses and how he confronts those possessed. In the exorcism narratives we are presented with an atmosphere of conflict and fight that is missing when Christ confronts illnesses. This is a fixed pattern. Evil spirit:

- Addresses Jesus defensively;
- Is aware that one has arrived who can defeat him;
- When ordered by Jesus to depart, seeks to avoid the attack, but eventually must give in to the stronger one, reduced to a last manifestation of fury and spite: *The unclean spirit convulsed him and with a loud cry came out of him* (v. 26). This shows us that the evil one is hard to overcome and that Jesus uses effort in an authentic combat.
-

The Gospel writer's intention is revealed in this narrative:

- To tell us that the deliverance from Satan is the sign that the kingdom of God is at hand (cfr Mk 1:15);
- To tell us that Jesus' Word is something new and powerful.

This narrative also has a Christological function:

- To awaken in the reader the fundamental question, the question that is asked throughout the entire Gospel of Mark, which was written to answer that question: *Who is Jesus?*
- And to offer the elements for a first response: *A new teaching with authority. He commands even the unclean spirits and they obey him* (v. 27).

The Gospel writer makes it clear that this narrative is open in two directions:

First: the exorcisms are constant in Jesus' Messianic activity. In fact, we see this in the first summary of this activity in the context of healing. In the second summary of this activity, we see it accompanying his preaching. Therefore, in the context of healing or in the context of preaching, exorcism is the constant. It is an essential part of Jesus' Messianic ministry.

Second: the narrative is not simply a victory over a demon, but rather a sign of general destruction. Note that he doesn't say, "have you come to destroy me", but rather "have you come to destroy us".

What does Jesus do in every casting out of a demon? He confronts and militates against the entire demonic army. When Satan says, "have you come to destroy us", he recognizes that the arrival of Jesus is the sign that ensures the definitive defeat of demonic powers in the cosmic and eschatological fight between God and the Devil.

Jesus is the holy one who annihilates the powers of evil. And when he says to Satan, "Quiet, come out of him", the Vulgate says "*Exi de homine,* leave man". This fact assumes a universal value. This does not refer solely to that man, but to every man, to all of humanity. In his ministry, Jesus reveals his mercy and has come to free, not just that man, but all of humanity from Satan.

Furthermore, unlike the crowd, the demons know who it is they are confronting. Thus, Mark uses them to reveal who Christ is: "I know who you are: the Holy One of God". Jesus forbids him to speak (the famous messianic secret). This restriction, nonetheless, does not impede that divulgation of the fact in itself. Indeed, it happened publicly, in front of everyone. There was nothing to forbid. Moreover, Jesus did not want the ensuing explanation of exorcisms to reveal his true identity. Much less does He want Satan to be the one to reveal it.

THE SECOND EXORCISM: THE GERASENE DEMONIAC

This is one of the most interesting exorcisms and it is the second recorded by Mark. The text:

They came to the other side of the sea, to the territory of the Gerasenes. When he got out of the boat, at once a man from the tombs who had an unclean spirit met him. The man had been dwelling among the tombs, and no one could restrain him any longer, even with a chain. In fact, he had frequently been bound with shackles and chains, but the chains had been pulled apart by him and the shackles smashed, and no one was strong enough to subdue him. Night and day among the tombs and on the hillsides he was always crying out and bruising himself with stones. Catching sight of Jesus from a distance, he ran up and prostrated himself before him, crying out in a loud voice, "What have you to do with me, Jesus, Son of the Most High God? I adjure you by God, do not torment me!" (He had been saying to him, "Unclean spirit, come out of the man!") He asked him, "What is your name?" He replied, "Legion is my name. There are many of us." And he pleaded earnestly with him not to drive them away from that territory.

Now a large herd of swine was feeding there on the hillside. And they pleaded with him, "Send us into the swine. Let us enter them." And he let them, and the unclean spirits came out and entered the swine. The herd of about two thousand rushed down a steep bank into the sea, where they were drowned. The swineherds ran away and reported the incident in the town and throughout the countryside. And people came out to see what had happened. As they approached Jesus, they caught sight of the man who had been possessed by Legion, sitting there clothed and in his right mind. And they were seized with fear. Those who witnessed the incident explained to them what had happened to the possessed man and to the swine. Then they began to beg him to leave their district. As he was getting into the boat, the man who had been possessed pleaded to remain with him. But he would not permit him but told him instead, "Go home to your family and announce to them all that the Lord in his pity has done for you." Then the man went off and began to proclaim in the Decapolis what Jesus had done for him; and all were amazed.

Christ comes to the region all of the Gerasene, a pagan territory. A man possessed by an evil spirit lives among the tombs, outside of the city. No one has been able to restrain him. He is broken, out of the senses, and violent. We can say that this is a disconnected man, dispossessed of his own faculties, no longer master of himself and has even become an enemy unto himself.

Note well what it says in verse 5: *Night and day among the tombs and on the hillsides he was always crying out and bruising himself with stones.* From being his own enemy, Jesus delivers him from Satan, who is sent into a herd of pigs who throws himself off a cliff side into the lake. Christ frees him and gives him back to himself.

The crowd marvels at the event and, nonetheless, asks Jesus to leave their territory. And so Jesus leaves. This too, we will attempt to explain.

The event closes with yet another surprising element. Jesus does not accept the healed man as his follower, but sends him to his own people so that, as Jesus says, he recount to them the great things that the Lord has done for him in His mercy.

This narrative is placed on the broad canvas of exorcisms, all bearing the same message. And what messages that? The evil spirit is hard to overcome and man is incapable of defeating him. Yet now, one who is stronger has arrived before whose word, not even Satan is able to resist.

The fact that Mark has placed this episode in a pagan territory is not irrelevant. The presence of the kingdom – note the meaning – is not limited to Israel's borders. The Gerasene demoniac is the proto-type pagan, who, after the Resurrection, will receive Christ. Thus, the episode is transformed from being a simple exorcism:

- Into the proclamation that the Kingdom of God is at hand;
- Into an evangelizing moment;
- Into a universal message: the good news and the power of Christ knows no bounds. It is universal.

With a similar expression to the possessed man in the synagogue, this demoniac addresses Jesus: *What do you have to do with me, Jesus, Son of the Most High? I adjure you do not torment me.* Yet again, Satan reveals his conviction that Jesus has come to destroy his power.

The deliverance from evil spirits is an essential part of Christ's mission. An attempt to remain in the region, by entering into a herd of swine, in reality does not turn out well or obtain the desired effects, but rather gives evidence of Satan's ruin. The unclean spirits, cast themselves off a precipice into the sea, where about 2000 of them drowned.

Subjugated by the resistible force of Christ, the demon is compelled to reveal his identity. His name is "Legion" because, as he says, "we are many."

The demon is one and they are many. We can refer to him in the singular and in the plural, in this passage, where the demon is identified as "Legion", he speaks in the first person singular. Pay attention to this, it is interesting.

On the other hand, in Mark 1:24, where it does not explicitly refer to multiple demons, the possessed man speaks in the plural, *What do you have to do with us? Have you come to destroy us?*

This discreetly suggests that in every casting out of the demon, the entire demonic army is cast out.

There is, moreover, a series of significant contrasts in this passage.

A) The first contrast

The most obvious is that demoniac himself. Before his encounter with Christ, he is a poor man, alienated and violent, anti-social and divided. He sums up all of the damage that Satan can bring about the man, who was made according to the image and likeness of God. Nonetheless, after the encounter with Jesus, the demoniac returns to his senses and finds himself anew. Marveling, the crowd sees him sitting down, dressed, and with his faculties (cfr v. 15).

Mark underlines the before and after element when he says precisely that he, the one who had possessed by Legion... The state of possession and the state of deliverance are set against each other. This is not a work of man; the villagers had already attempted many times. This passage underscores the power of the Word of God.

Satan's hallmark is precisely man's alienation, the loss of all of his relations. The Gerasene demoniac is the personification of "non-relationality", that is contrary to man, because man, by nature is a rational and relational being. Precisely here we find the negation of this relationality.

This negation "appears" – writes Enzo Bianchi – in the man himself, in others, and with life. Evidence is given in his nudity. In his wondering among the tombs and the mountains, dwelling among the dead, exhibiting self-destructive behavior that compels him night and day to strike himself with rocks, alienating him from all social relations."

What a stupendous explanation that highlights the devastation that Satan brings about in man, who is precisely made according to the imaging and likeness of God.

The hallmark of the kingdom of God, on the other hand, is the reconstitution of man. The possessed man rediscovers his dignity. This passage says that he was dressed and back to his senses. From animal-like screams, he is brought to humble supplication, asking Jesus permission to become one of his disciples. Whereas the first rejected the encounter and communication with Jesus, screaming out with loud voice: "What do you have to do with me?" And now, he manifests his desire of a relationship with Jesus, asking to remain with Him. Whereas the former man lived among the dead, now he returns to the living. In his mercy, Jesus restores him to full freedom, He heals them, and He integrates him in all of his relations: with himself, with his relatives, with society, and with God. All of these relations have been compromised by the devastating work of the Devil.

Whereas Satan, makes man evil, and even possesses him; Jesus frees him, make some good and, in the case of the Gerasene demoniac, restores him to freedom through obedience, doing what Jesus says. Here we find in Mark's Gospel, the first missionary in pagan land.

B) The second contrast

In this passage we are presented with the following: Jesus is stronger than Satan and it is capable of doing what the crowd was not capable of bringing about. They have frequently tried to restrain him with chains and shackles, but the possessed man reduced them to bits, and no one could restrain him.

The crowd recognizes Christ's power, yet at the same time fears Him. They are confronted with a threat. Something that ought not to bother them does indeed bother them nonetheless. And so they come to Him, asking Him to leave their territory, in spite of what Jesus has done. He is rejected. Apparently, the crowd expected in deliverance of different sort. The deliverance that Jesus brings about is not simply a return to the way things used to be in its human element; but brings with it something new that arouses rejection, and He doesn't demonstrate a minimum of opposition.

It is surprising to contrast the way in which Jesus confronts demonic opposition and human opposition.

Confronted with demonic opposition, Jesus fights it and comes out victorious; confronted with human opposition, Jesus surrenders. He reveals a certain strength and weakness that go along together, here, we find the shadow of the Cross.

In spite of his victory over Satan, the remains, nevertheless, residual opposition, a hostility that Jesus does not try to defeat. As a result, Satan's opposition perdures in men's darkness. Of himself, Satan would have no power, because he was vanquished by Christ. If he does of power, it is because he finds accomplices in the hearts of men. Christ has defeated Satan and cast him into the sea among the heard of swine. But the victory of His Word, nonetheless, is limited by the incredulity of the habitants of the Gerasenes. As a result, this disaster among pigs does not mark his definitive destruction. Rather, it pre-figures it.

C) Third contrast

Among the various contrasts, we find the behavior of Jesus in relation to the man whom He has delivered. He does not accept him as a follower, but sends him back to his own people. Jesus distances Himself from the place, but leaves there the testimony which again, according to the Gospel, to spread throughout the Decapolis: the great things that Jesus had done for him, leaving everyone in awe. With this, the passage closes.

In this way, Jesus leaves, but He does not leave. Even the incredulity of the Gerasenes is unable to hinder the power of His Word that has overcome the evil spirit.

It is important to remember that this encounter is not a lesson in demonology. Mark's Gospel does not present a demonology. Rather, it is theology, Christology, anthropology. This important episode about a possessed man is also an important lesson in soteriology, Christ who saves.

D) Fourth contrast

To close this part we will underline to more aspects.

The first describes the movement of deliverance in all of its trajectory: far from Christ and dominated by the evil spirit, the man is alienated from all human interaction, experiencing internal divisions. The salvific action of Christ undermines the dominion of Satan, reconstitutes the man and introduces him into his Kingdom, making love him a new man.

The second regards newness: the people feel threatened, disturbed, compelled to resist the Word that liberates. And so, Satan who has been defeated by Christ, finds in the heart of man a new opportunity to oppose the Word that has defeated him. Nonetheless, in sight of the incredulity and rejection, the liberating Word is proclaimed by those witnesses who have been able to receive it.

THE EXORCISM OF THE POSSESSED BOY

What follows is an encounter Christ had accompanied by Peter, James, and John.

When they came to the disciples, they saw a large crowd around them and scribes arguing with them. Immediately on seeing him, the whole crowd was utterly amazed. They ran up to him and greeted him. He asked them, "What are you arguing about with them?" Someone from the crowd answered him, "Teacher, I have brought to you my son possessed by a mute spirit. Wherever it seizes him, it throws him down; he foams at the mouth, grinds his teeth, and becomes rigid. I asked your disciples to drive it out, but they were unable to do so." He said to them in reply, "O faithless generation, how long will I be with you? How long will I endure you? Bring him to me." They brought the boy to him. And when he saw him, the spirit immediately threw the boy into convulsions. As he fell to the ground, he began to roll around and foam at the mouth. Then he questioned his father, "How long has this been happening to him?" He replied, "Since childhood. It has often thrown him into fire and into water to kill him. But if you can do anything, have compassion on us and help us." Jesus said to him, " 'If you can!' Everything is possible to one who has faith." Then the boy's father cried out, "I do believe, help my unbelief!" Jesus, on seeing a crowd rapidly gathering, rebuked the unclean spirit and said to it, "Mute and deaf spirit, I command you: come out of him and never enter him again!" Shouting and throwing the boy into convulsions, it came out. He became like a corpse, which caused many to say, "He is dead!" But Jesus took him by the hand, raised him, and he stood up. When he entered the house, his disciples asked him in private, "Why could we not drive it out?" He said to them, "This kind can only come out through prayer" (Mk 9:14-29).[3]

---

[3] Before handing the word over to Bishop Costanzo, I ought to clear up something very important: it Is not true that the boy described by Mark, according to many biblical scholars, is suffering in epileptic attack. There are attributes that point to a diabolic possession. For example:

In this exorcism we discover three stages:

- First: Jesus encounters the crowd and has a first dialogue with the boy's father;
- Second: the demoniac is presented to Jesus and Christ speaks to the father second time;
- Third: the exorcism and the dialogue that Jesus has with his disciples.

The narrative structure demonstrates that the Evangelist is not so much interested in the exorcism, as he is in the dialogue that Jesus has with the father and His disciples.

---

1. Mark makes it clear distinction between sicknesses and diabolical possessions, between the power of healing and the power of casting out demons.
2. Jesus, who has the power to heal any illness, would have simply done so, without having recourse to exorcism: "Deaf and mute spirit, I order you, leave him and do not return." If you were dealing with a case of sickness, as many scriptures scholars maintain, it is inexplicable that he should use an exorcism, telling the demon to leave the boy.
3. Nor can we believe that Jesus was mistaken in his diagnosis, confusing a diabolical possession with the physical illness. That would compromise his divinity.
4. The issue of throwing himself into fire and water, as the father describes, is not part of the symptomology of epilepsy.
5. The conclusion of the passage explains why the disciples were incapable of freeing the boy: "this type of demon is only cast out with prayer", which wouldn't make sense if this was merely an illness, and not a diabolical possession.
6. Finally, admitting but not granting, that the boy was an epileptic, one ought to remember, as we exorcists experience frequently, there are pathologies that have natural causes and their apologies that are caused by demons: the latter we call diabolical vexations, that are healed, not by way of drugs – something that would render no fruit whatsoever – but by exorcism. The gospel speaks of a mute, and a woman bent over for 18 years. Hereto, Jesus has the power to heal, but he uses exercising, testing out the demon. And having casted out, the mute begins to speak and the woman can stand up straight. Here we're dealing with pathologies caused by a demon. So, granting that the boy was having an epileptic fit, one ought to at least recognize that here there is a pathology that is not natural, caused by the demon. By way of exorcism, Jesus took away that illness. Having cast out the deaf and mute to spirit, the boy regained his health.

While Jesus was absent, his disciples attempted to free the possessed boy from the mute spirit, but were unsuccessful. While the disciples, the crowd, and the scribes stand there arguing, Jesus appears. The boy's father intervenes, explaining: "I asked your disciples to cast it out but they were unable." Literally, "did not have the strength", so they were incapable. And this becomes the beginning of a two-sided dialogue with Jesus, highlighting three affirmations regarding the faith.

The narratives true theme is, clearly, faith in the order of salvation, understood at its roots, as deliverance from the demon, and in relationship to his disciples who, in the time of the Church, would continue the salvific mission of their Master.

The two concluding verses seal the episode with an explicit ecclesial dimension. They are a pastoral teaching for the community with clear reference to exorcisms and those who practice them.

From this point of view, the episode is conclusive, because it unites the two lines, that of Christ, whose word is powerful; and that of his disciples do whom He confers the same power. It also demonstrates that the time of Jesus and a time of the Church are in continuity, yet conditioned: by faith.

To the disciples who ask the reason for their impotence, Jesus reminds them of two things. He reminds them about prayer, just as earlier He had reproved them for their lack of faith (v. 19), adding that anything is possible for him who believes.

Faith is the only road to victory over Satan, because the victory belongs to God and not to man. Man can make the victory his own only inasmuch as he is faithful and obedient. Hence, the reason an exorcist ought to have recourse to prayer: he ought not trust in his own powers, but in the powers of God.

The tyranny of Satan loses vigor and it is immediately defeated precisely there in the encounter of obedience and faith. He rediscovers his lost strength when man trusts in himself.

THE STRONG MAN AND THE STRONGER MAN

We continue our reflection on the Gospel of Mark.

The name "Satan" occurs in mark four times:

- In the temptations in the desert (Chapter 1)
- In the discussion with the scribes (Chapter 3)
- In the explanation of the parable of the sower (Chapter 4)
- In the remonstration of Peter (Chapter 8).

A) The temptations in the desert

The Marcan narrative is quite simple: the Holy Spirit drives Jesus into the desert. Jesus dwells in the desert for 40 days, tempted by Satan. He lives in the wilderness among wild beasts, while angels serve him.

As we can see, Mark is not interested in the explicit nature of the temptations and the trial to which Jesus is submitted. Nor is he interested in the development of the temptations, or how Christ overcomes them. The narrative, rather, seems to dwell on one fact: it is concerned with the surroundings of the event. Moreover, everything that follows in this Gospel reveals the precise nature of the temptation, its development, and Christ's success. Mark is only concerned with telling us simply that Jesus, after his baptism, was tempted. The link between baptism and temptation is evident: "Immediately after his baptism the Spirit drove him into the desert". The link between baptism and temptation is explicit and intentional. As a response to the baptism, in which Jesus receives the Holy Spirit, there is a return to the desert, that is, to an existence in which the struggle with Satan ensues, but not without the Father's help, who sends angels to minister to Him.

These are the two coordinates between which the entire existence of Jesus develops. On the one hand, Satan attacks Him; and on the other, the Father helps Him, precisely because He is obedient and faithful to the Father.

B) The discussion with the scribes (Mk 3:20-30)

This discussion with the scribes is important, because in it Christ offers a theology of his exorcisms and their explicit Messianic role.

Since they cannot deny his actions, what are his adversaries to do? They seek to discredit him in his actions and in His Person. Their attempt:

- They say that His exorcisms are the work of magic, used to seduce the crowds;
- He casts out demons through the power of demons;
- And further, He is possessed by a demon (v. 22).

Confronted with such explanations offered by those who are specialists in the Law, that is, the scribes, the crowds are perplexed. Christ rebuts with logic, "Satan cannot act against himself", and offers the most obvious explanation of his work: "someone stronger has arrived, the Messiah, who has overcome the strong man, that is, Satan".

Everyone knows that the kingdom of Satan will be vanquished in dawn of the eschatological age. "Indeed," says Jesus, "those times are at hand". *No one can enter a strong man's house to plunder his property unless he first ties up the strong man. Then he can plunder his house* (Mk 3:27) demonstrates that Jesus considered Satan as his personal nemesis whom He must overcome to bring men to God. Jesus' exorcisms speak of this victory. Not a mere healing of symptoms, but a removal of evil at its roots. Far from partial victories, he anticipates the total and definitive victory with these signs.

C) The remonstration of Peter

The motivation behind Satan's activity is expressed quite clearly in the remonstration of Peter (Mk 8:33). Jesus says to Peter: "You do not think as God thinks, but is man thinks". Satan attacks in order to dissuade Christ from the messianic path laid out by the Father, that is to avoid the way of the Cross, abandoning the divine salvific plan. Here are the essential contents of the temptation that confronted Jesus and that he continually overcomes.

The first temptation in chapter 1, of what did it consist? It was made up of a threefold expression whose purpose was to dissuade Christ from following the loving design traced out for Him by the Father, the salvation of man. Christ does not accept it. Each time he appeals to the Word of God and casts out Satan, who left for a while – until the established time of the Cross.

The entire life of Christ was a "yes" to the Father, and a "no" to the tempter. He lived in obedience from beginning to end, revealing clearly that He vanquished the Evil One in virtue of His loving obedience. Love reaches its fullness on the Cross, "the Cross of Christ". On the Cross of Christ the power of the evil spirits was broken through the power of love, a love that takes everything upon itself. Here is the power of Christ, sent by the Father: in His total conformity of will. As we can see, the entire life of Christ, from beginning to end, was submitted to the will of the Father:

- Entering into the world, He said: "Father, behold, I come to do your will" (cfr Heb 10).
- At the well, he told the Samaritan woman: "My food is to do the will of him who sent me and to bring it to completion". (Jn 4).
- In the Garden of Olives he prayed: "Father, if it is possible, let this chalice pass; but not my will, rather let your will be done."

THE THEOLOGICAL AND ANTHROPOLOGICAL FRAMEWORK IN MARK

To deepen and appreciate theological and anthropological framework in Mark, we ought to place much of the data that he offers us in their proper and presupposed context in which they move.

The belief in demons and in diabolical possession was a common cultural fact for Jesus, the Evangelists, et al. Where one might expect to encounter an exuberant demonology, one finds, an uncommon sobriety in its exposition. One does not find speculation about the names of demons, their hierarchy, their dwelling place, their nature or the nature of their sin. Nor does one find a theoretical or speculative interest in demons. And this is so throughout the entire New Testament.

Mark's Jesus has not come to reveal the secret nature of evil spirits, but to announce that God has taken charge of our confrontation with the evil. It is precisely He who takes charge in the confrontation with evil. As a result, Mark's contention is threefold:

- To demonstrate the nature of man in need of redemption;
- To explain the sense of Jesus' mission;
- To Illustrate the dangers experienced by the Christian community.

Mark's data according to a historical-salvific outline

We can order the data Mark offers us primarily according to a historical – salvific outline: the time of Jesus and the time of the Church. With His obedience, Jesus has vanquished Satan definitively at the roots. Nonetheless, and Satan continues to be the tempter:

- He takes the Word from the heart of man (cfr parable of the sower);
- He impedes the disciples from understanding.

This is valid for the entire New Testament in every passage in which it speaks about the fall of Satan; to the "now" is joined the "not yet". Given the Satanic threat, nothing is definitive:

- Neither in the heart of man that is easily misled. The Psalmist says "an abyss, a chasm... the heart of man is an abyss";
- Nor in the pagan world which has become the mission field for Christians and a place that can give testimony to God's wonders (the Gerasenes ask Christ to leave);
- Nor among His own disciples: we have already seen how He reacts to Peter.

Satan continues to attempt to slow down in its path the Word of God that defeats him:

- Taking advantage of the incredulity of the Gerasenes;
- Taking advantage of the incredulity of the disciples;
- And above all, tempting the Messiah away from the crucifixion.

Peter believes in the Messiah, but does not accept the crucifixion, and, as a result, receives the title Satan: *Vade retro, Satana*. As if to say, "Take your place as a disciple, this is my road, not yours".

Satan, tempting Peter to separate the Messiah from the Cross, the victory over evil from the way of love and obedience, he seeks to obtain from the disciples that which he could not get from Christ.

For all of this, the discourse on Satan takes place in the context and the arrival of deliverance, along with an urgent exhortation to constant vigilance: *Fratres, sobri estote et vigilate, quia adversaries vester* etc....).

In any case, in the time of the Church, Jesus' victory over Satan remains possible. Jesus, in fact, sends the disciples to announce the kingdom and to free men from the power of evil spirits. In order to free them from evil spirits, there are two conditions, so says the Gospel: with faith and with the way of the Cross, precisely that which Satan opposed. Satan tries to distance man from the way of obedience and commitment; Satan masquerades as self-sufficiency, as worldly wisdom, and thus impels man to count on himself, and to take to the road of power and self-discovery. When this takes place, Satan reveals his power and dominates everything. Whoever has experience of the heights of the spiritual life, especially the mystics, will recognize this hallmark in their dealings with penitents and other people in spiritual direction.

Mark's data according to a split that goes from symptoms to roots

In a historical – salvific outline, we can order Mark's data according to a sort of vertical split that goes from the surface to the core, from the symptoms to the root.

Jesus has come to undo every form of demonic influence. More profoundly, Christ meets Satan precisely there, where he can divide man.

The true place of Satanic presence is not in sickness, that is merely a symptom. The true place of Satanic presence is in the depths of man's core. It is possible for Satan to nestle there, bringing about all sorts of disturbances, marring man's true identity, destroying all of his relationships with God and anyone else. This was apparent in the pages of the healing of the Gerasene demoniac.

But Satan expresses himself, taking possession of man in more painless ways: pay attention, because this is more frequent now. Satan take possession of man in forms that are less painful than sickness, in much less dramatic ways: for example, in his indifference before the Parable of the Kingdom, in his rejection of the Cross. These are not the harshest ways that Satan takes possession of people, but rather are quite subtle: it has to do with a demonic power that distances one from God, with deceit and worldly wisdom. "You think as men think, not because God thinks", He said to Peter (Mk 8:33).

Mark's unfolding data regarding a theological reading of human existence and history

The data that Mark offers us, reveal, a true and proper theological reading of human existence and history. The exorcisms in Mark intend to present us simple cases that exemplify our own situation as sinful man, at the mercy of the forces of evil and incapable of entering into communion with God.

The exorcisms points to a state of man's perdition without God and his permanent condition as one who was exposed to temptation. As the rest of the Bible, Mark conceives of man as a unitary being, belonging to God in spirit; in the deep core of this person, such as in his relations and in external manifestations.

And the dominion of Satan strikes man in body and in soul, in himself and in his relations with the others. Healing and exorcism are not two juxtaposed things, or different signs. Rather, man's existence is strictly bound to God, and it is uniquely in the acceptance of this relationship that this becomes a liberated existence. Hence, the reason why the contrast is not only between God and Satan, but as well the contrast between man and Satan.

Conjoined to the glory of God, what is at stake is man himself, his integrity, his freedom, and the possibility that he has to separate himself from obedience to the Lord. Here the anthropological implication is the acceptance of an existential project that brings man to give himself to God in the acceptance of the way of the Cross. In separating himself from obedience to the Lord, man mars his own identity, the structural principle that unifies and harmonizes him. The face of the demon is confusion, alienation, disintegration, in which he wants to involve man.

The contrast between Christ and Satan reveals, finally, a vision of history. What is this is history? It is a fight between good and evil, whose protagonist's are not only the forces of nature nor merely simple men, but God and the Evil One. This is an opposition that occurs on three levels:

- The contrast between Jesus and his opponents;
- Between Jesus and the possessed;
- Between God and Satan.

This thought is not proper to Mark alone, but is found throughout the entire New Testament.

Biblical man is of the opinion that the calculations of history do not turn merely on natural events and the forces of nature, man, and God. There is also a malignant force. The fight between good and evil involves man, yet is beyond him, and can only be resolved through God's intervention. Nonetheless, man's responsibility is never subtracted from the equation.

According to Mark 7:20-23, Christ does make men's sins reducible to the devil, but to the heart of man, from which they spring; from within that heart of man He uncovers all of the beautiful merchandise therein contained..... our evil thoughts.

Jesus' exorcisms do not assure man of anything, but rather put him in the condition to choose.

THE INVOLVEMENT OF THE DISCIPLES IN JESUS' EXORCISTIC ACTIVITY

To conclude this chapter we are to consider a line of thought that regards everyone, but above all exorcists.

A quick reading of The Gospel of Mark reveals to us that His itinerary involved the disciples in His exorcistic activity.

The first four to be called are together with Jesus in the synagogue of Caphernaum (Chapter 1). And in there, in the synagogue, there are present at the first exorcism performed by Jesus.

Later, after the Pharisees and the Herodians have agreed on His death (Mk 3:6), Jesus establishes the Twelve, to be with Him – the first thing; and the second, to follow him in his ministry of preaching and combating demons: *that he might send them forth to preach and to have authority to drive out demons.*

After the scandal of his mission at Nazareth, Jesus sends the Twelve on mission, two by two, conferring upon them, so says the text, authority over unclean spirits. Therefore, that to which they were called is about to take place. They quickly understand the efficacy of their mission, preaching, casting out demons, and healing the sick. They are sent by Jesus, his mandates, his Apostles (Mk 6:6-12).

The Apostles in their mission assimilate to themselves that which is of Christ: preaching, casting out demons, healing.

By way of the Twelve, Jesus continues his own mission. This assimilation is born out particularly in exorcisms.

But after their return from the mission, there is a certain hardening of the heart in the disciples: they become obtuse, they seem to have appropriated the blindness of the incredulous whom they were to evangelize. After the confession of Peter: "You are the Messiah", Peter is reproved because he is tempted by Satan, opposing the fulfillment of God's design, rejecting the Cross, refusing a suffering Messiah (Mk 8:31-33).

The last exorcism is actually and existential statement about the Twelve. They are powerless to cast out the unclean spirit from the possessed boy and show how much distance there is between them and Jesus, refusing to enter into the mystery of the passion. Further, they are incapable (literally, "without strength") of carrying out the task that Jesus had destined them for, having conferred upon them power over unclean spirits.

We are confronted with a parable of descent: those who were called to be with Jesus end up abandoning him.

Those who were invested with power to cast out demons, something they had powerfully exercised before, are reduced to impotence.

From descent to collapse.

And in light of their incapacity and impotence, every extraneous exorcist is put in high relief. Take a look at this scene: a man, who does not belong to the circle of disciples, casts out demons in the name of Jesus. The Twelve show up and even want to prohibit him because, as they say, "He doesn't follow us, he is not one of us." Sectarians in defense of group privileges!

Yet the impotence of the disciples confronting the possessed boy becomes for Jesus an occassion of judgment and an opportunity for teaching that has true catechetical value.

The boy's father has brought his son to Jesus, saying that he asked His disciples to cast out the unclean spirit, but they did not have the strength to do so. And Jesus says: "*O faithless generation, how long will I be with you? How long will I endure you?* The disciples' impotence directly reveals their lack of faith. In fact, immediately after that Jesus says, "for him who believes, everything is possible". If you are not able to do so, it means that you do not believe, hence their ability to deliver a perverse generation, inability to believe in God and obey his Word.

Jesus, disgusted by His disciples' inability to believe, tired of granting powers to disciples who render them sterile for their lack of faith, unleashes on them a Moses-like cry to Israel: "incredulous and perverse".

The dominance of evil, expressed by Satan, reveals that man is radically impotent to free himself. He is only capable of doing so when he entrusts himself to God, to whom everything is possible. And Jesus shouts: "Everything is possible for him who believes", bringing about a paradoxical cry from the possessed boy's father, "I believe".

Entering into the house – an ecclesial space – he is asked in private by the disciples about the why of their impotence. Jesus says: *This kind can only come out with prayer*. Here we have the weapons indicated by Jesus for the deliverance of a demoniac: Faith and prayer. There are no other weapons.

I would like to remind you that there is an ancient gloss, attested to in many codices, which adds fasting, as well.

Therefore, since the exorcism is efficacious, Jesus indicates the means for us: faith, prayer, fasting. These three means ought to be accompanied by a profound humility and an attitude of compassion for the man, who, once freed, is restored to God, with the ability to love Him and give witness to Him.

Part II
Testimonies

Fabio: rescued from Satan thanks to the prayer and support of a community

Friar Benigno (FB):

Fabio was one of the gravest cases that I've ever had. He came to me for the first time on November 27, 2013, accompanied by a priest who, initially and prudently, was skeptical about the possibility of this being a case of diabolical possession. With time he had to accept this reality.

In our first encounter he told me that already at 10 years of age he heard a woman's voice calling out to him seven times. From that moment onwards, his nightmares were constant and he saw what appeared to be dead people. One time, someone who claimed that his name was Antichrist told him that God did not love him. Further, if Fabio did not commit himself to him his mother would die before his 16th birthday and he would be at fault. Shortly thereafter his mother died.

Frequently, while asleep or trying to sleep, the covers would be torn off of him. He also related how his participation in Mass increased his disturbances.

One time his mother brought him to a psychic seeking help for her son. After this encounter, he experienced levitation for the first time, something that his mother witnessed.

As soon as I began the rite of exorcism he entered into a trance and a new personality emerged. Commanding the demon in Latin to tell me his name, something he refused to do saying, "I'll never tell you!" and became extremely violent. During the exorcism of October 2, 2014, upon commanding him in the name of Jesus to tell me his name, he replied, "Lucifer, Asmodeus, and Legion."

To help me with this case, I had a medical team made up of a criminal and forensic psychopathologist, two general practitioners, a psychologist, a psychotherapist, among others, all of whom were witnesses to the exorcisms and all that occurred during the prayer. They were unanimous in declaring this a case of diabolical possession.

To gain a broader perspective of what occurred during the exorcisms, we will hear from various participants. One team member, Stella, was present at every exorcism and accompanied Fabio during those long years.

Stella: It all began the day before, when he when he became peevish, disturbed during the celebration of Mass, manifesting invective towards the priest who offered the Mass, mumbling to himself, saying that things were just going to get worse for him because "the other one" did not want to see Friar Benigno, but he knew that he would find some relief, nonetheless.

In the evening he began his desperate vigil: he began to send me rambling texts, which were an inarticulate jumble of words and punctuation, an authentic chaos in which the only intelligible words were those of self-denial elation and death. His obsessive writing mentioning that all of his attempts at suicide would end in nothing but that this evening he would finally have success, leaving me a last farewell with these words: "No one except my mother has ever loved me, she's dead and I'm all alone. You cared for me but you can do nothing to help me. Father Matteo La Grua cared for me and help me, and even protected me within his monastery but when he left us, I had to go. I have no other future. This is my destiny."

A few minutes later he would call me on the telephone seeking comfort, inquiring about my silence. I told him that I did not respond to his texts because I was praying. Then he attempted to give me the impression that my prayer was actually bringing him great comfort and that I should be very proud of myself, but it was clear that the devil was making a laughable attempt to make me proud. Then he began to speak at an intellectual level that was far superior to his own culture, as if it were a dissertation, citing chapters and verses of the Scriptures, referring to facts from the lives many saints, comparing himself to them and, in fact, putting himself far above the greatest of saints. Then he began to claim that his state of possession was actually God's plan to save many souls because he was heroically offering himself as a victim for their salvation. Of course he did not expect to find any contradiction in me, and how could there be, since he had such a superior knowledge of the Scriptures and of history as his discourse was displaying, never missing a reference to book, chapter and verse of the Bible.

All I could do was tell him that Jesus loved him and that I had entrusted him to the protection of the Blessed Mother. At that point, his voice became cavernous and guttural, spewing out all sorts of disastrous predictions of the future, which in hindsight, never came to pass.

Seeing that he failed to scare me, he then changed his tactic, delighting in the lurid details he cooked up regarding all the priests that he had met wandering from church to church, from one priest to another. Since I did not know any of the priests he mentioned, I began to look them up on the internet. One of the priests he had mentioned was Friar Benigno, whom I had never seen or heard of before. In my own naïve imagination, I supposed that an exorcist ought to be tall and strong, with the sort of brawny build one needs to battle such powerful creatures. What did I know of exorcism or exorcists except for those images from movies that I couldn't get out of my head?

Returning to Fabio: Of course he knew much more about these things than I did, and he would tell me how every night before an exorcism he was punished with insomnia, desperation, vexations of every sort, and when he did manage to fall asleep it was restless and filled with nightmares ending with beatings and marks on his body, feeling the pain deep into his bones.

When we would meet at the place where the exorcisms were performed, and as we awaited his turn, he became agitated, unapproachable, aggressive, he would scream out, fall to the ground and become stiff as a board. The courtyard near the entrance of the building was covered with rough gravel and he would fall on it so hard but we could never find the smallest scratch on his skin. As soon as Friar Benigno's secretary would call him for his turn he would try to escape and act like she didn't know who we were or where he was. He would look deep into my eyes. But they were not his eyes: his pupils dilated so much that they were indistinguishable from the iris and they had a flickering glow, almost like a car blinker. His fingers would then stiffen, and then close into a fist, arcing the first and last fingers in such a way that it, left the palms exposed. He would always break out into a heavy sweat, even on the coldest of winter days.

Once he was brought into the room where the exorcisms were performed, he was helped onto a mattress and five strong men with stand by to intervene in the moment in which his violence became superhuman. He always outdid himself!

As soon as Friar Benigno approached, and before a word could be said, Fabio was thrown into an uncontrollable fury, contorting his body, whipping his head around, doing everything to wrest himself from the hands of those who restrained him.

Although my eyes were closed as I try to recollect myself and pray for Fabio, I could hear the grunts, screens, the maniacal laughter, but could only imagine the faces he was making and the large quantities of vomit and phlegm but I could hear being expelled from his mouth, as his body moved on naturally and powerfully.

Only once was the pattern of behavior different. Fabio appeared composed and relaxed on the day that he came for an exorcism, as the friar who received him and began to speak with him in a friendly manner. They looked like two old friends conversing. After a bit of small talk, with lightning light fury and completely unforeseen, since there were no prior signs of alteration, he lifted a table with one hand in order to bring it crashing down on the friar, but was restrained by some friends who accompanied him and thus began one of the most disconcerting exorcisms I've ever witnessed.

Fabio fell to the ground and slithered like a snake while the friar began his prayers. It became impossible forcibly to immobilize him, since he was able to park his body, legs, and arms with such great elasticity, in a way that defied the limits of human physicality, that his friends were incapable of securing either his arms or legs. Once he subdued by the strong arms of his friends, he escaped in an instant and grabbed the friar's habit shouting: "Shut up, pig. Do you really want me to leave? I'll leave but only to come after you! Your prayers are so boring! How I love those priests who celebrate Mass quickly, who love the things of the world, who give Communion in the hand to those who bring it to me!" Immediately after this, he began to shout in desperation, "Leave me! Leave... He's here, next to me. Get away from me."

FB: "Who should leave?"

Fabio: "Him, that black crow."

FB: "Is the Black Crow Father Matteo La Grua?"

Fabio: "Yes, get them out of here. Get out, leave, you're hurting me."

FB: "Father Matteo, intercede for Fabio. Come to his aid with your intercession."

Fabio: "I'm going to kill you! You're a dead man."

FB: "Who are you going to kill?"

Fabio: "You. You're a failure. Follow me and I'll make you be rich and successful. You'll be someone. You don't understand anything, you boring old man."

FB: "That's true. I am a failure in the things of the world, but I have a treasure you will never have: the love of God! And now I order you, in the Name of Jesus Christ to tell me you are."

Fabio: "I am Suedomsaaaaaaaaa."[4]

FB: "Who else is with you?"

Fabio: "Lucifer."

FB: "And?"

Fabio: "I am Legion, stupid priest. Enough."

FB: "Fabio, I consecrate you to the Blessed Virgin Mary. Blessed Virgin Mary, come to help this your son, crush the ancient serpent!"

Fabio: with a fixed gaze, squealed, "No! Nooooooooooo... Not her!. Leave me, leave me!"

FB: "Who is she? The Blessed Virgin Mary?"

---

[4] Asmodeus backwards.

Fabio: "Yes, it's the woman. Terror of all of hell."

FB: "Virgin Mary, come to the aid of Fabio with your intercession."

Fabio: "The lady is on her throne. Not her! Not her! I'm leaving.... Stop!"

After the right of exorcism, not having achieved the definitive deliverance, friar Beningo invited us to pray the rosary while he sprinkled Fabio with holy water, touching him with a crucifix and relics, which sent Fabio if into such a violent crisis that the five strongmen were no longer able to hold him down. The cries of this lamb sent to slaughter resounded against the walls in the ceiling of the small room.

I don't know how much time had passed when it seemed that he was calm again and was able to join us, albeit with an audible voice, in the recitation of the Magnificat. Having finished the exorcism, we all set our goodbyes and exchanged embraces when all of a sudden Fabio exploded anew. All resumed our positions, some praying, some physically restraining Fabio, and Friar Benigno praying his exorcism rite, glancing over to the demon possessed Fabio saying, "I won't stop crying until you leave."

And that's how it was. Fabio, after the recitation of the prayers indicated by the rite of exorcism had been recited, contorted himself and looked like a dying man emitting his last breath. His eyes, which were completely jaundiced, rotated back to their normal position, and he said: "It's okay, help me to get up. I can't get up on my own, I'm exhausted." He was free, if only for a little while.

And now we will see how Fabio's liberation took place. In Stella's words:

I knew Fabio from two years back, having met him at the Church of our Lady of Mount Carmel, in the country outside of Palermo. That's where life and brought me at that stage, although now I live in a different part of Sicily and attend a different parish. Ever since our Lord has called me to conversion I've learned to savor the things of God, but I must admit that my lively imagination does not always know how to distinguish those things that come from God and those things that come from my own mental construct.

Walking into the church during one of the daily Masses, at the moment of consecration, my mind was filled with an image: the Blessed Virgin Mary was suspended over the altar and a black horrible cloud covered her face. I mentioned this to Father Vincenzo but he did not give it any importance.

A little time past and, seated in the last pew, I noticed the young man who seemed quite nervous, indolent, agitated, crude. He was clearly losing it. I noticed that he was always accompanied by one or two parishioners at his side. I wondered about all of this, but then thought that it wasn't my business to inquire about somebody else's suffering, and other people were taking care of him. Little did I know that this young man would enter into my life of faith like a hurricane.

On New Year's Eve two years ago I organized a dinner at my house, having prepared everything before hand so that I could go to Mass. Taking the last dish out of the oven, I spilled the contents of the tray on myself and all over the kitchen. With this mess I figured it didn't make sense to leave the house, but a powerful interior impulse took charge, making me not worry about the scalding burns and so I cleaned up the mess I had made in record time and ran off to church.

There, during the praying of the *Te Deum*, I saw that strange young man, the one who was always in the last pew. But this time he was running down the center aisle of the church: his hands were behind his back, with a menacing and mien, eyes filled with hatred. As he approached the altar I feared for the celebrant, but two strong men intervened and shepherded him towards a side aisle. I felt great compassion for him. He looked like a child tossed about by waves, almost at the point of drowning. I experienced an inexplicable maternal love for him, almost as if my heart wanted to give him all of the help that he needed.

At that moment the police asked the entire congregation to pray for the young man who is tortured by dark forces. Could he be possessed? I thought. Up until that time I had always entertained strong doubts that demons could take possession of people, even though the Bible speaks about it and confirms this reality. I just assumed that he was a mentally disturbed young man, but Jesus invited me to love him and this is what took hold of me in that first moment. Not knowing him, I wasn't sure how to go about asking Father Vincenzo how I could help. While I was asking him how I could help this man, he told me that he had already been thinking that I was somebody who could help Fabio carry his cross.

And that's how this odd relationship began, although the more I got to know him, the more he gave me the impression of being a psycho – a psycho whom I loved in Christ.

Every morning Mass it was the same: my task was to pray and Fabio had the hard part: agitation, coughing, falling to the ground unexpectedly, blackouts – all of this in the last pew so as not to disturb the congregation during Mass. It was a spectacle and no tickets were needed. Sometimes I was really exhausted because he was so aggressive, other times all I could do was laugh at the oddity of it all. He even laughed later when I told him what happened, because he had no recollection of what had occurred.

Devil or psycho, we were a good fit and I would tell myself that regardless of which one he was, the Lord would work his miracle if we asked with all our heart. My prayers for Fabio were constant as I tried to help him on a human level. He had many bad friendships that he did not know how to get out of, because they were his only source of survival from the moment that he lost everything: his parents, fraternal affection, work, stability. Consequently, it was necessary to be even more giving and generous than his false friends. And since good done silently makes more noise than evil done bombastically, I chose that route. Besides the priest, I was the only person close to Fabio, who had burned bridges with all of the Christians who had supported him in various parishes and towns.

As soon as Fabio was ready to relate to me something of his experience, I was bombarded with all sorts of details regarding his possession: things that happened in his childhood, curses, dealings with tarot card readers, his many sessions of exorcism with various exorcist priests, his sense of delusion having trusted some people who claimed to be Christian but who acted differently. In an almost obsessive way he would repeat that he never would have confided in me had he not cared for me.

His emotional behavior towards me was extremely varied: one day he would seek me out, another he would hide from me, other times he would smile at me, and then he would seem to detest me, at times he was very talkative and other times I couldn't get a word out of him. These alterations were from one moment to the next, regardless of the circumstances. One moment he would vibrate with euphoria and suddenly turn suicidal. He would laugh hysterically and shortly thereafter fall into a deep depression and anger, not as if he had two different personalities, but a thousand faces. All of this made me think that he was schizophrenic, something I attributed to the terrible misfortune and tragedy of his life.

Nonetheless, our relationship grew closer and more solid and, for his part, he showed an ability to have a growing correspondence manifested in a growing delicate conscience and little sacrifices. He began to seek me out in the most critical moments and began to trust me, calling me by my name, something that he had never done before. He showed fear of being yet again abandoned, but would nonetheless entrust to my confidence all of his problems, disappointments, and the problems that came along with being possessed – visions of demons, fixations, inexplicable accidents what happened in his house and all sorts of horrible things that happened to everyone around him, telling me that I too would have to pay the price for being close to him like so many people before him. At that time in my life everyone in my family endured trials and illnesses of all kinds. Fabio stressed that all of this was owed to his presence in my life and if I would simply give up, all of this would come to an end for us.

Of course I would hear nothing of that, but rather offered all these crosses to the Lord for the healing of this young man who, according to me was "sick in the head."

It became evident to me that his personality was broken in two: there was a Fabio who had a good heart, who was generous, sensitive; and this would be replaced by a Fabio filled with hatred, rancor, contempt, and given to calumny. I begin to think about the fact that insane people are always insane, following the twisted and false logic of the insane, while the good Fabio reasoned within the parameters of an irreproachable and sequential logic. As a result, doubts about my evaluation of his insanity began to arise and I began to feel guilty for not having given faith to the words of the exorcists who had helped him.   Have confirmed that this was a true case of possession I would have to take that possibility into account. Further, I could not fail to take into account the passage of the Gospel of Saint Luke in which Jesus frees the demoniac. *And after his deliverance the people saw that he was dressed, of sound mind and seated at the feet of Jesus (cfr.* Lk 8:35). This passage suggested to me that the lines of demarcation between possession and insanity are not always clear for us, but Jesus took it upon himself to clear up all of my doubts.

One afternoon, as we were participating in Mass with great difficulty because of his constant agitations, he looked at me with eyes that seemed to emanate fire any said to me in a guttural, cavernous voice: "Look at those two, I hate them so much I could kill them right now." I turned around and I saw two young men who looked like everybody else. Shortly afterwards the priest said that we had the pleasure of having two seminarians at our Mass and he pointed to the two young men who are the object of Fabio's rabid hatred. Father Vincenzo would later confirm that there was no way that Fabio could have known who they were, since he was the only one there who knew about their presence. At that moment I had to ask the Lord pardon for having doubted the words of so many priests who had sought to help Fabio and, together with my husband, I began to accompany him and his sessions of exorcism with Friar Benigno, praying ever more and offering works of mercy for the good of the soul of this young man who took up an important place in my heart.

Fabio began to ask me counsel on how to fight against the demons who had ruined his life thus far, but I was at a loss for what to tell him since I could find no words, not having the sufficient experience and certainly never having been trained in the service of combating evil. So I would simply pray and be attentive to what Christ showed me and I would relate it to Fabio. The Lord never abandoned me and Father Vincenzo has always supported me with prayer and constant presence.

Although the sessions of exorcism increased it did not seem that they were bringing much benefit to Fabio. So many hopes of deliverance were extinguished just as often and the state of possession continued and it seemed that this would last his whole life long. This was precisely the devil's weapon: the loss of hope and the conviction that good is stronger than evil. And so more prayer, more works of mercy that feed faith and hope. Every once in a while Fabio claimed that he was delivered, but it was a deception, a diabolical strategy which was not difficult to see through since he lacked humility and intended to put himself at the center of everyone's attention even though he seemed to have an impeccable Christian behavior in church.

One time the following occurred during an evening of Eucharistic adoration. Fabio, having escaped from me, finally came back and sat next to me and started telling me how embarrassed he was to create such a spectacle in church and he was tired of being taken for a madman when after all it was the devil was doing this to him, especially while he was in church. Little by little, through difficult times and not so difficult times he struggled to take control of himself: he trembled, perspired, raised his fist to beat me. But in the presence of the priest who processed through the aisles with Jesus in the Blessed Sacrament, all hell broke loose just as it happened during the exorcisms. Four strong men struggled to bring him under control such was his violent aggression. I was next to him and I beseeched Jesus to come to our aid and I found a strength I never knew I had, along with a great desire to embrace him and hold him close with maternal instinct. Fabio's fury was placated and replaced with such a calm that he seemed he fell asleep. From that evening onwards, I noticed a progressive improvement and a more determined will in Fabio to take charge in this battle for his own deliverance from these chains that held him.

I could write a book about all of the days I spent with Fabio, since each one was his own adventure. But foremost in my memory are the last battles in which I was present for some of the Lord's prodigies.

One day while I was praying in church, an image of the Blessed Virgin Mary came to my mind. She was banishing that dark and monstrous figure that I had seen before. Around that time Fabio told me that he had a dream and also a "sensation", as he called it, that on a certain Friday something important would happen and I would need to be there to help him. Of course it was difficult for me to distinguish between what was true and what was false since there were so many predictions that turned out to be simply lies from the devil. Consequently, I do not know why that prediction gave me such joy and fed my hope.

We continued praying together, going to Mass every day, receiving Jesus and the Blessed Sacrament, and he seemed to be getting better, albeit still quite attacked. During Mass on July 29, 2016, Fabio suffered a severe attack. He became agitated and was launched from the pew towards the altar before which he fell, convulsing, and then became rigid. It was a Friday and I remembered what he told me, that I would have to help him.

I did not know what it meant to help him in this situation or what I was supposed to do, but I went to him keeping my husband close to me because I was aware how violent and powerful he could get. I knelt in front of him and asked him if this was the Friday when he needed my special help and he nodded "yes". I had the sensation that's the devil was impeding his speech and so I asked him if this was the case. He nodded once again. I asked if he would protect me from the devil if I were to touch him and he nodded a third time, still unable to speak. Meanwhile, Father Isaiah was offering Mass next to Father Vincenzo. I caressed Fabio's face, then put my hand on his heart telling him, "Fabio, shout what it is you want. If you ask help from Jesus the devil will not be able to stop you." "Jesus, free me" were the words he was able to formulate, but only with superhuman effort. But they were enough. With that, he was able to get up and walk upright, smiling and no longer hunched over.

When Mass ended I accompanied him to the tabernacle only to hear this heavenly melody: "I, Fabio, renounce Satan and all of his seductions." My shock was so great but I could not experience either joy or wonder. Deep within me I had the certainty that a miracle had occurred, but I would have to wait till the next exorcism for Friar Benigno to give me the certainty that it was so.

During the prayer of exorcism, unlike the other times, Fabio did not enter into a trance, nor did he have any reactions, but rather was able to join us in prayer without the least difficulty. A profound peace accompanied us all during the prayer. Subsequent sessions brought about no reactions, and his daily life was without disturbance – so many of which I had witnessed. It all stopped.

One thing remains foremost in my mind.

Since July 29, 2016, Fabio has changed completely. The love that unites to Christ remains the same, but Fabio is a new man from the inside out. He has broken every link with temptation, destroying pictures and objects that had any sort of relation with his past life of sin.

Another change in his life is that Fabio has finally gotten to know me. Before, he never knew my last name, but now he can't ask enough questions about my life. When I asked him how it was possible that in the last 2 ½ years he would never show any interest or curiosity about this person who was with him almost constantly, his response was quite disconcerting: "I was used to living in darkness and I only saw the dead people. Although I cared for you, it was very difficult for me to be aware of the living."

Everything I have written about my experiences with Fabio is a brief synthesis, and very little in comparison to what Father Vincenzo went through, never sparing any charity or prayer for him. Fabio, who loved Father Vincenzo from the start, sometimes seeming to hate him, calls him "the priest of my heart."

My odd, unique and sometimes adventurous service for Fabio has not ended. He has become a trusted friend for whom I continue to pray, albeit not for his deliverance, but for his vocation. I have always ardently desired that one of my sons would be consecrated to the Lord. Perhaps this is the one....

FB: We conclude giving the last word to Fabio himself.

Fabio

Friday, July 29, 2016.

In my parish, Our Lady of Mount Carmel, in the outskirts of Palermo; during Mass, more precisely during the consecration of the bread and wine, I endured a strong fight with the devil. I sensed deep within me that this would be the last battle, at the moment of the Elevation. It was precisely in that moment that I received the definitive deliverance after so many years of torment. And all of this thanks to the ceaseless prayers of so many brothers and sisters in our community. From this experience I have grown to understand how important it is to be close to a community, a community that I have always sought.

Nonetheless, the devil tried to keep me far from the sacraments and even though he succeeded in bringing me to live in an abomination before God, the smallest flicker of the flame of faith was never extinguished.

I lived as if I were drugged – doing and saying things out of my control, against my will. I was surrounded by psychics and other people who lived far from God. I considered myself the son of Satan more than of God, since I did not love the light and I always sought darkness. I couldn't take, or better said, I hated and rejected everyone who dared to come close to me to give me a little love. And in spite of it all, that little flame that the grace of God gave me for my salvation impelled me to fight and renounce Satan, seeking a community that would help me.

I remember that when I was in a trance, whether it worked during an exorcism or during Mass, I often saw the Blessed Virgin Mary and, right next to her, Father Vincenzo, parish priest of our Lady of Mount Carmel.

I am delighted that he was the one who helped me reach deliverance. He never did prayers of deliverance for me, never participated in the prayers of exorcism that Friar Benigno offered. But the devil hated him so much because in his silent prayer, with his charity and with his love, just like the Blessed Virgin who lived in silence, accompanying of the community in their prayer, and in a special way those brothers who accompanied me during the sessions of exorcism and prayers of Friar Benigno, who always received me with a smile, profound affection and goodness, breaking those chains that had me bound up to the evil one for so many years.

It is so important to be a part of community. Love can do anything, especially the love of Jesus that lives in the hearts of one's brothers.

And how could I not thank Father Matteo La Grua, who from on high was always near me during the exorcisms and continues, even today, to guide me. A few days before my deliverance I dreamed that he came close to me commanding Satan and all of his legions to depart from my body.

Mario: rescued from the trap of a Satanic ritual

FB: Mario's case illustrates for us the fruits of one's poor choices, especially those choices which gravely offend God – thus opening all sorts of doors and windows, giving the devil free access to enter the life of man in an extraordinary way.

My first encounter with him was on March 14, 2014. In the initial intake interview and discernment he recounted the following:

Mario: along with a group of adults who formed part of a Satanic cult, I thought I would play along. One afternoon I was with my friend Angelo. After walking around town a bit he suggested we go to a place near Cefalu, in the Province of Palermo. He said that on that night a Satanic sect was meeting. It picqued my curiosity very much and I accepted the invitation, unaware what I would encounter. We arrived at the place indicated and Angelo presented me to the leader of the sect, who explained to us what we should do and, above all, what we should ask for during the ritual.

We went inside and found a small, semi-dark room. There I saw things no one should ever see. On the table I saw a woman of about 40 years old, naked. I was told she was a white soul, "a pure and immaculate victim", who would be offered to the devil. On the walls, written in blood, or phrases such as, "I am your god", adore Satan you have all that the world has to offer", "666, I trust in you."

The group was made up of ten men, all hooded except for the leader who wore a long habit. And so the ritual began. They all positioned themselves around the woman and began to pray in a language I had never heard before. Then they recited the *Hail Mary* and the *Our Father* backwards, frequently invoking Satan, with hopes of being heard.

We all cut ourselves with knives and our blood was poured into a chalice which was placed next to the nude woman. Immediately thereafter, that chalice was offered to Satan and everyone, one after another, with the exception of Angelo and me, had sexual relations with the woman. Around the woman there were seven lit candles. Everyone began to blaspheme the name of God. As the ritual continued a Ouija board was brought into the room, upon which were certain Satanic symbols and the letters of the alphabet. This was used to communicate with the spirits. Everyone, Angelo and I included, began to invoke Lucifer and all the other demons. In that moment I saw a Lucifer in the form of woman who said, "power, riches…" and I made a pact with him. I gave him my soul. In exchange she had to give me money, sex, and power. Shortly thereafter, the Ouija board was taken away and we began to drink the blood that was in the chalice.

Having drunk some of the blood I began to feel very cold. I heard cries of desperation and I saw written on the wall: "I am the one that you have invoked." Not being able to bear any more of that horrible spectacle, Angelo and I escaped, bringing with us the Ouija board that had been left outside.

From that night onwards my life became hell: I blasphemed day and night, hearing voices compelling me to kill myself or to kill others, constantly desiring a barbarous sex. I had continuous visions of women inviting me to have sex with them and I experienced a repulsion for all things holy. That's when I began to smoke marijuana and to drink.

FB: Mario came to meet with the priest who was entrusted with the task of spiritually accompanying him, a certain Father Damien. After Mario had told me everything that is related here, he turned to Father Damien, saying, "Father I'm at my wits end what should I do?" Let's listen to Father Damien and see how he helped this young man.

Father Damien: I have always been aware, more from books and articles than anything else, of the harm that come to people, unawares, from insane curiosity. I knew well that curses are real and that they could cause harm to spiritually weak people, but I never had first-hand experience with anything close to what happened to Mario.

In spite of having read a great deal about the subject, I can say that it is one thing to read about certain things in books, but quite another to have direct contact with those things. Now I believe more than ever that the devil can possess people in order to eternally damn them, and that in order to address these serious and grave cases, well-prepared priests, who are spiritually strong, are needed to combat to evil one.

I am a priest, but not an exorcist, and I was not able to address Mario's case with the specific prayers of exorcism. In spite of that, counting on my priestly ministry, the first help I could offer Mario was to pray for him and with him

We began praying the holy Rosary, but by the time we got to the third mystery, Mario began to contort himself in his chair, his face took on an evil aspect and his eyes became like fire. He stopped praying suddenly, the devil was coming to the surface. Mario's voice started to become cavernous and scary. It was no longer in his. And then he began to insult me, telling me to leave that soul because it belonged to him. He moved up with such fury and violence making it very difficult for me to try to restrain him. I began to have serious concerns about my own safety.

I returned to prayer, invoking the Blessed Trinity with lots of faith, imploring the Blessed Virgin Mary and St. Michael the Archangel. I allowed the insults and the verbal attacks to fall into the void as I understood that this was a grave and serious case. I knew I did not have all of the means necessary to help Mario. I knew we needed an exorcist and Friar Benigno, whom I knew new very well, would have to take the case.

Without losing any time I contacted him and we made an appointment. While driving there in the car I began to have my doubts that Mario's case was a real diabolical possession. I think it was an inspiration of the Holy Spirit. I asked for light and began to pray the holy Rosary in silence. Up until that moment Mario had been calm, but at that point he began to get agitated and feel sick.

"What's going on?" I asked.

"I feel horrible all of a sudden. A moment ago I was fine and now I feel very disturbed. I don't understand it."

I no longer entertained any doubts.

To Friar Benigno's prayers of exorcism, the devil manifested with all of his strength and the malice, with endless hatred for God. When commanded say his name, the response was Beelzebub and Coral. I saw and heard things I've never experienced before: such horrible blasphemies, screams and insults against Friar Benigno and me. The strength that erupted in Mario was superhuman: for strong men could not manage to restrain him. When the friar commanded him to leave, he responded: "No, I'll never leave, you ugly bastard. Mario is mine, he belongs to me." The more we pray, the greater the cries, and the more his strength diminished. Holy water, a crucifix, relics of Padre Pio, and the Miraculous Medal – such were the weapons that Friar Benigno used during his exorcisms. I realized that precisely these instruments - often undervalued and even subject to banal rationalism – form a part of our way of faith. They are useful and powerful in the fight against evil.

In all of the subsequent exorcisms I would add, to what I have already related, that the spit mixed with blood that came out Mario's mouth was perhaps the blood that Mario had drunk some time before, after he had given his soul over to the devil in exchange for money, sex, and power.[5]

The encounters with the exorcist took place every two weeks and, with Friar Benigno's consent, I would pray with Mario at his house, obviously without saying prayers of exorcism, since only an exorcist may use them. On September 20, 2014, with the help of two friends, Mario and I begin a novena to St. Michael the Archangel.

---

[5] True enough. Often, the objects expelled during the exorcism are related to the genesis of the problem. Such manifestations seem to represent the enemy's laying down of certain weapons.

These were nine days of physical and spiritual suffering for Mario, but his desire to be free was such that he bore it all with patience. Mario began to take his path of faith seriously. The fundamental and indispensable means for his deliverance were Sunday Mass, weekly confession, and constant prayer. At the same time, he began to distance himself from friends and acquaintances, anyone who had anything to do with the occult or Satanism. When Satan was attacked through prayer Mario's crises augmented notably. Even his relationship with me fluctuated. Clearly, the devil was trying to put a wedge between us.

In the summer of 2014 I decided to take a trip with him to Medjugorje,[6] something that infuriates it the devil and became abundantly clear to me. One Sunday, while at my mothers house, I decided to take a nap. It was interrupted by a phone call from one of my parishioners.

"Father Damien, I need you."

"What happened?" I asked.

"My daughter," he said, "she's bad, disturbed. She's destroyed everything in the house and is speaking a language I can't understand."

"I'm not an exorcist, but anyway, bring her to the parish. I'm on my way."

---

[6] It must be stated that the Church has not yet made a definitive statement on this phenomenon.

There, in the parish I saw Sylvia. She couldn't stand, her eyes were glassy and she moaned with a cavernous voice. I had them let her out on the carpet and I began to pray the holy Rosary. Upon invoking the Blessed Virgin Mary, Sylvia began to writhe and scream, so I put my hands on her head, invoking the Holy Spirit. The demon within her said to me in a threatening tone: "You're not taking anyone anywhere."

I didn't know what he meant or what those words referred to, so I continued to pray. After a while, Sylvia became calm, coming out of her trance and was able to go home with her husband. I stayed there asking myself what those words meant. That afternoon I went to have a pizza with Mario and his parents. As we were at table speaking about nothing important, the conversation turned to the pilgrimage to Medjugorje. Mario suddenly became agitated and was taken by a panic attack. Leaving the restaurant quickly, he went into the corner of a garden and begin cough up blood, and get all agitated. At a certain point the devil manifested and, looking at me, said with a threatening tone "You're not taking anyone anywhere." Mario wasn't supposed to go to Medjugorje. This was the meaning of the words that came out of Sylvia's mouth. What should I do? I was afraid of not being able to handle the situation during the pilgrimage. Friar Benigno counseled against his going.

The most direct experience the devil that I had was when I decided to take Mario on vacation for a few days so he could rest. Our relationship was one of father and son. After the first day, which was serene and relaxing, we went back to the hotel. Before going to bed I went out onto the balcony to pray my rosary. Mario asked if he could join me in prayer. I said, "Okay but if you begin to feel badly tell me and we'll stop." By the second mystery he began to experience disturbances and I suggested we stop praying. "Continue," he said, "I want to win this, not him." I continued. He did everything he could to not leave, but by the third mystery it was no longer Mario. "Lord, help me, I'm all alone and I don't have the strength to handle him."

Meanwhile Mario had fallen out of the chair onto the floor. I picked him up and placed them on the bed and continued to pray.

I called the Holy Spirit down upon him ... and a storm let loose. As usual, he began to writhe about on the floor where he was falling, spitting up blood and aiming insults at me. After praying for 20 minutes the devil took a break, but not before forcibly shaking Mario, telling me: "I'll leave for now but at 3 AM I will come back and you won't sleep all night."

Mario came back to himself, got up from the floor and asked what happened because he was feeling lots of pain. I only told him a little of what happened and he said, "Okay, let's go to sleep." He fell asleep immediately but I didn't even have the courage to turn out the light. At 3 o'clock precisely, he turned his head towards me, snickering: "Hi, priest. Still awake? Well, here I am, just like I told you."

I threw myself on top of Mario to hold him down as he became agitated. "Stop, stop, I don't want to fight with you. Let's have a chat about this." Then, with rage he added, "Mario belongs to me, he's mine." And then he began to scream, "he promised me his soul, he sought me out, I didn't look for him – he looked for me and I gave him everything he asked for: power, success, money, and so much sex. Sex and prostitution are my greatest temptations with people. Do you know how many people I win over with these sins? I'll never let Mario go, he is mine and he will be in hell with me."

Then at one point he turned his head to the left side of the room, as if someone had just arrived. Then, turning to me, he said: "Your dad's here (he had died that same year), do you want to speak with him? I can let you speak with him, if you want." Then, with a sarcastic tone, he said to me: "You know, when people don't believe in me or, out of curiosity, play certain games, I delight in that, because I can work without being bothered. When you speak with Mario about everything that happens when I manifest, I enjoy that. It piques his curiosity and the possession becomes deeper." From that moment onwards I would never speak of it again with Mario.

And then with fury he added: "I'll make your life impossible, I'll send so many people to you that you'll never have peace, by day and by night. You and that other idiot tired me out with your prayers, but I'm not moving. Mario is mine and I will never leave him." And letting out some screams, he left the young man.

FB: With the exorcisms repeated every two weeks, Mario began to get better little by little. His disturbances began to diminish until they completely disappeared, but this would take two years of exorcisms. In the last exorcisms there were no reactions to the prayers. He's doing fine now. Mario goes to Mass regularly without the least difficulty. He is very conscientious about his regular confession and Communion and dedicates time every day to personal prayer.

Aurora: freed during an exorcism through the intervention of the Blessed Virgin Mary

My name is Aurora. Unfortunately, I became acquainted with the Evil One in my young years and experienced its consequences in the most brutal and tragic way imaginable. It is invaded every aspect of my life with such arrogance and in ways unexpected, when I thought I had everything, when I thought that I could desire nothing else, when I felt strong and rich, unaware that I was only rich in futile and material things that only brought me material pleasure but distanced me more and more from God, the God who always loved me, even onto giving up his life for me. But I was ignorant of him, and not having God in my life, thinking myself rich, I was actually the most indigent person in the world.

The evil one entered into my life almost as soon as I meant the man who would become my husband, but especially when I got to know his family, whom, so it seemed, I could never please. Perhaps it was owed to profound possessiveness or even a certain jealousy that his mother had for him.

Our story began in the year 2003, shortly after the death of my father. I was 22. Our entire relationship was rife with his mother's hatred for me, her distorted selfishness, and a certain morbose love for her son. Since I was not the girl she picked for him, and even though she did not know me, I could not be the right life companion for son. Instead of seeking her son's happiness, she began to suffocate him.

Unfortunately, this rejection from the start brought with it lots of tension and awkwardness in a relationship and even brought about in her son violent reactions towards me – always at her behest. As a way of defending his mother, he began to attack me and this was what brought about an interruption to our story for five long months.

After those months he returned to me, asking pardon and promising that he had changed, telling me he wanted to marry me. He claimed that he had detached himself from his mother because she was too possessive and wouldn't allow him to even breathe. He promised me we would form a family and his mother would not be involved.

With the hopes that everything would be as he said I accepted the proposal and we decided to get married in 2007, against all odds and, especially, the will of his mother. With that day came my own condemnation to unhappiness.

It was a mistake in marriage and nonexistent from the very beginning, lacking a solid foundation. It was built on empty promises. From the first day our marriage was the object of his family's hatred and attack, not only trying to come between us, but also trying to convince him to leave me.

There was never a peace in our house, nor love or mutual respect. Every day was a civil war with heated discussions and verbal attacks until such point that he decided he hated me, blaming me for all of the misery we are undergoing from his family.

We became isolated little by little. His parents refused to come to our house if I was present and if I was in their house they refused to recognize me, as if I wasn't there. My husband acted as if he did not notice this, acting as if nothing were out of the ordinary.

Of course there was a total rupture between me and his family, but he continued to see them, as if he were unaware of the harm they were doing me.

He would receive gifts from them that he would bring home, such as plants that he would immediately transferred to our garden. A friend of his family, a woman who apparently treated me well, would always bring me various foods, especially fresh eggs, for me to eat. Unaware of the evil intentions behind them, I accepted these gifts as a gesture of good will and ate them.

As days and months and years pass, things got worse. It reached the point of violent abuse and my life became one of tears and sorrow.

Around this time I began to have certain disturbances and physical maladies. I was bothered during the night and on the following morning I would wake up with scratches and marks on my neck and my chest. He would ask me what I dreamt about because he told me that he would have to fight to take my hands from my neck as I attempted to strangle myself, but I remembered nothing of that, in fact I didn't believe him and I laughed at him. The strange thing was that none of this really caused me any fear, nor was I curious to find a solution.

As time passed I no longer felt I needed to pray or go to church, or to ask for help. I was convinced that I could confront this thing alone. The only desire that burned within me was the thirst for revenge. My only feeling was hatred and rancor against everyone and everything.

As the situation got worse, so did my health. Each day my abdominal pains increased and I experienced frequent vomiting and inexplicable hemorrhaging, causing me to have to stay in bed since I couldn't move anymore. In spite of this it was of no concern to me that my desire for revenge possessed me more and more each day against those who had always bested me and always seem to stay several steps ahead of me.

By now arguments were a daily thing between my husband and me. We had one that took place in front of his parents right in their home - it was furious and out of control. My husband was inhuman in his treatment of me, I remember crying so much because of my fear, while his mother, instead of shedding a tear, stoically watched me, without the least surprise. Rather than reason with her son, she sat there, immobile, enjoying the scene is it were the movie, waiting to see how it would end. As she watched me, she smiled, as if to say, "I won." A few days after that tragic event, our marriage broke up definitively. That was February of 2011.

I abandoned our house and, in order to avoid further violent attacks, every once in a while I would return to take some of my things. Crossing through the garden, I remember the rose that his mother had given me and, in a rabid fury, I tried to kill it, throwing acid on it. The more I tried to harm it, the more it flourished. I told myself I would destroy it when I came back. But when I came back it was too late because somebody else had already taken it away.

We began the legal process of separation. And in every session with the lawyers I had to sit with that man who hated me so much, now just as much as his family had.

From that day onwards my life became one of absolute sorrow, my eyes always filled with tears and darkness inhabited my heart. My health deteriorated day after day and I was subject to much suffering.

Some of my friends saw me in this condition so they invited me to participate in a certain Mass which would be celebrated that evening, if I felt better. In spite of all of the reasons not to go to the Mass, I decided in favor of it.

As I stood before the church I remember that my legs began to shake and, once I was inside, I began to cry ceaselessly, without knowing why. I didn't stop until Mass was over.

The priest began the celebration of Holy Mass and I remember how his look bothered me. It was as if he never took his eyes off me. During the Eucharistic procession along the main aisle of the church, he at first walked past me, but then spontaneously turned around, holding Him before me. Suddenly I couldn't breathe.

When everything was over I tried to explain it away to my friends, but the priest approached me and, coming close to me, whispered; "You need help….. The Lord be with you."

I ignored him and went home continuing to not only miss Mass, but to do all sorts of stupid things that young people do to keep themselves busy: stay out late at night, leading a life deprived of order and direction, until that fateful day when something very strange occurred.

I was at home and I had a picture of my deceased father in my hands. I cried and asked him with all my heart to help me find away out of the suffering, because I was tired and I wanted to experience a little happiness.

I cried more tears than I thought possible, so much so that it was difficult to open my eyes. But once I did, I saw a large drop of blood in my right hand. Frightened, I ran to the bathroom look in the near. I couldn't find any wounds on my face and my eyes were clear. I touched the drop with my other hand, cupping it in my palms. I ran downstairs to the family that lived under me and told them everything that it happened. At first they didn't believe their eyes or no my words.

Aware that those who heard me did not believe me I began to cry in desperation and fear. And suddenly, once again, but this time in front of everyone, when I wiped my face with a white handkerchief it was stained with blood and once again no wound could be found on my face and my eyes were clear.

At that point they were all in shock and began to believe me, asking one another what they could do to help me.

The next day I spoke about this with a dear friend of mine who helped me reflect on how I distanced myself from the Church. She asked me to reflect on why, regardless of all of the things that happened to me, why did I think I did not need to come closer to God and pray. She asked me also to reflect on what turn of events had come about so that I never set foot in a church. I, on the other hand, knew well. The very thought of it frightened me. That's when we began to speak about some Franciscan friars whom her mother could introduce me to in Palermo, in the San Isidoro di Baida neighborhood. She spoke about a certain friar Francesco Pio, whom I had met a long time before in that same church, before the death of my father.

Thanks to them I was able to meet this friar once again, but not in Palermo, rather in Corleone. I experienced great joy when he remembered me after so many years. He also spoke of my father.

My first step was to go to confession, something I hadn't done for years. Until this point and that they could open up certain doors to the Devil. I committed one: before getting married I participated in a séance in which I was convinced that I spoke with my dead father, not knowing that it was actually a demon.

After the confession, before leaving, the friar invited me to pray the rosary everyday, but he noticed a strange reaction in my face that made him suspicious, even though I was unaware. So he asked me to sit down again for a prayer, taking his rosary in his hand and putting it upon my head. During that prayer I begin to sweat and feel a very sharp pain in my stomach, and I began to cry and scream.

I returned to Corleone and several times more always accompanied by family to receive prayers of healing and deliverance, which always made me ill, sending me home full of anguish.

Unfortunately at the end of one of these prayer sessions, my sister sat next to me as the little friar places hands on my head. As he prayed in the low voice, I ended into a trance and I began to verbally assault him, but he wouldn't stop, on the contrary, he prayed more intensely for me.

At that point friar Francesco Pio understood that he could do nothing for me but would have to entrust me to an exorcist who would have to examine my case in order to see what was needed to help me. Among the names that he suggested to me were Friar Benedetto and Friar Benigno, both exorcists. For logistical reasons I decided to go to Friar Benedetto who at that time was in Palermo.

This was 2012. I arrived a few minutes early, filled with anxiety, incredulous and trembling, accompanied by my sister and my mother who had accompanied the friar in his prayers, and was always ready to help them when there was a need.

We were received a few minutes after the established appointment time by him and one of his team members who participated in the prayer. He brought us into a little room in the monastery, where there were some chairs, a couch and on the walls a few pictures of angels and saints.

Friar Benedetto had me sit down in a little chair and before he sat down, he approached me and placed a long violet stole on me, with a prayer book in one hand and a crucifix in the other. The crucifix had a medal of St. Benedict embedded in it. He sat down next to me and began to pray the Litany of the Saints.

My family recounts the following:

Friar Benedetto: he started to pray.

Aurora: I started to cry.

FB: he began to recite the exorcism.

A: Still and silent, I began to sway and a stretch my arms, like somebody was just waking up.

FB: He continued to pray.

A: I begin to mumble "…..mmmmmm….." and to sway about in the chair.

FB: He sprinkled me with a little holy water.

A: I began to scream louder and turn my head so as not to see him, I began to shake and shout.

FB: He asked, "Who are you? Tell me your name."

A: No response, just screams. And so it continued to the end.

FB: He concluded the exorcism praying a *Hail Mary*.

I returned home without remembering anything, experiencing all sorts of pain in my body and filled with anguish. The other exorcisms took place every two weeks and they were always very hard on me.

My family recounts the following:

FB: After the initial rites, he began to recite the prayer of exorcism.

A: I began to cry and sway about in the chair again, eyes down, and then I raised my head to look at him and, as if to get his attention, cried out, "Priest…. Priest."

FB: He ignored me and continued his prayers, not giving me any attention or importance..

A: There was great pain in my voice, "Priest…. Priest…. Can't you hear me?"

FB: "Leave her…. I command you in the Name of Jesus."

 A: I began to become very nervous and with a loud scream said, "Noooo! She's mine!"

FB: "She belongs to Jesus….. Tell me your name."

A: I didn't respond but after a while of silence, with a look of intense hatred for him, an evil and cavernous, subterranean voice said, "What do you want from me, priest?"

FB: "Be quiet... I asked the questions here..." Then he sprinkled me with holy water.

A: I screamed and jumped out of the chair, holding my stomach, crying out; "Eeeeeeeee!"

FB: He placed a relic of St. Pio on my stomach and on my back.

A: I let out a scream and attempted to bite his hand as I rolled about.

FB: He anointed me with blessed oil and closed the session with a *Hail Mary*.

I returned home but at that time I remembered nothing; simply feeling demoralized and lost, and all the while a voice within me continued to repeat: "There is no hope for you." I was never more convinced of this than then.

The days after the exorcism I was compelled to remain in bed on account of the pain in my bones and the horrible feeling throughout my body. It was as if a bottle of anguish in my heart had broken open, filling my whole being.

A little after that I managed to get somewhat better but the improvement was only temporary.

Day after day after my health declined. And then the constant fevers began that seemed impervious to antibiotics. The fever seemed to get better, only to return stronger than ever, accompanied by an inexplicable increase in bodyweight. Thus I was compelled once again to remain in bed, away from work and social life, left alone with nothing but my suffering.

But deep within I knew that I wasn't really alone, since someone or something was thinking about me in every moment of the day. And the strange phenomena that was occurring in my house was proof of it. I found lights turned on I would suddenly turn off and vice versa. And every night I had the same dream: someone whose face I could not see would sexually assault me.

I can't count the nights that I had to get up to turn out the light and how many mornings I woke up feeling dirty and violated for what had occurred. When I was finally able to, I recounted everything that was happening to me in the house during the night to Friar Benedetto.

I remember very well the expression on his face as I told him everything: he was very pensive and nodded his head, as if this were not the first time that he had heard somebody tell him all of these things, even in the details.

The following exorcisms were extremely violent and difficult for me.

What follows is a narrative by my family:

FB: After the usual initial rites he began the prayer of exorcism.

A: As usual, I began to sway about in my chair. And then I began to spit on him and to insult him, saying: "shut up, Priest. Shut up." And I writhed about.

FB: He prayed and prayed - always with great insistence. At a certain point he said, "Tell me your name?"

A: "No."

FB: "You're Asmodeus, right?"

A: I emitted an inhuman cry and began to speak in a strange language, rising from my chair.

Everyone present attempted to stop me because I had a superhuman strength. That's when the real fight begin.

FB: "Leave her, I command you in the Name of Jesus." He continued to pray and to sprinkle me with holy water.

A: "No, the bitch is mine."

FB: "In what part of her body are you?"

A: My belly began to distend.

FB: "I order you to vomit."

A: I attempted to vomit something out but nothing came up.

FB: He concluded this umpteenth exorcism having an idea which demon he was dealing with.

During the following days Friar Benedetto asked me to pray so much, to go to Mass every day, to fast, to confess frequently, to take Communion. How much suffering I had to go through to do all of that!

My family tried to bring me into church, sometimes by force, but every time I had to go, obstacles arose. I always sat in between my family members and had to engage in a true battle against myself at the beginning of every Mass. Spontaneously every hatred in the world was born within me, and this hatred was so ferocious and violent – hatred towards everyone and everything, especially the priest offering the Mass. And then I descended into a profound anguish. The Eucharist was like a burning coal in my mouth, sticking pins in my tongue, and I could only cry until the end of the Mass to the wonder of everybody present. Finally, at the end of the Mass I was always so embarrassed on account of how I had carried on.

Returning to my house I would often experienced such a furious hatred that it blinded me. This phenomenon was taking place with evermore regularity, especially if somebody got me angry.

When I was alone in the house the outbursts were extremely violent. I remember running into the bathroom to look at myself in the mirror and swear at myself: I let out threats, punching and kicking the mirror in the wall. I would end up beating up myself, punching and slapping myself while a voice urged me to kill myself. Sometimes I would find myself in the kitchen with a knife in my hands on the point of plunging it into my stomach where I experienced the greatest hatred, but suddenly and inexplicably, my eyes were opened and I felt great fear, throwing the knife away, just weeping until I finally calmed down again. Yet this calm was only apparent, since even more violent attacks awaited did me. I could never bring myself to tell anybody about these tragic and violent attacks and all of the things that were happening when I was alone, perhaps out of fear, perhaps out of shame, perhaps so that those who cared for me would not worry about me.

After a while Friar Benedetto was transferred from Palermo to Corleone, in the diocese of Monreale. My name was added to the list of the others that he had been helping to be handed over to the new friar who would substitute him: Friar Benigno. I waited and waited for the call from the new friar, but it took months - for bureaucratic reasons - as Friar Benigno awaited the mandate of exorcism that he had requested. In the meanwhile I continue to see Friar Benedetto in Corleone, but only sporadically given the distance, and the sessions were brief since the drive back was so long.

Since I began to feel desperate I wrote a letter to father Gabriele Amorth, telling him everything that had happened to me in my exorcisms with the Friar Benedetto. I needed his help. On March 13, 2013, to my great surprise, I received a response from him. With great hope in my heart I opened the envelope, which contained a little card with a hand written note:

> "Aurora, you have set out on a good path. Continue with confidence because the Lord rewards faith. Even if we do not see each other I will entrust you to the Hearts of Christ and the Blessed Virgin Mary.
> I Bless you in Jesus and Mary,
> Gabriele Amorth.

At first I felt very let down, because I thought that he would accept me and help me, not realizing, on the other hand, how much help and comfort those few words written in his own hand would prove a guide for me in my life.

In the following months I knew no peace and was subject to hard trials, going in and out of the hospital. At first the doctors couldn't figure out what I had. The fever states we're becoming regular and spontaneous. After the umpteenth intense night of fever, they diagnosed a spontaneous and inexplicable kidney blockage and began to give me antibiotics to try and save my kidneys, although the doctors seemed skeptical.

In the following days the fever began to come down and I still remember this stupor of the doctors when they told me that they were able to save the kidneys.

I returned home and it seemed that things started to get better, but spontaneously and without explanation, my health began to deteriorate again obliging me to undergo an emergency intervention to save my kidneys.

After that things took a turn for the worse, until the day of the great verdict in which we all had to except what I was fearing: they diagnosed a horrible illness called endometriosis, the sickness whose origins are unknown and seems to feed off of a woman's menstrual fluids. It seemed to affect the various vital organs. It proceeds similar to cancer and I was told it was classified as the fourth stage, the most grave. According to the doctors, this classification was based on the extension of the illness, given how much it had spread in the wounds left in its wake. In my case it had already effected the reproductive organs, the uterus, the rectum, and the stomach walls. The lesions that had been left were very grave and all of this happened in a brief time. The doctors spoke clearly to my mother and me. He counseled an immediate intervention that might be risky for my life. After the surgery I had to take a pill that was still in the experimental phase called Vissane. It put me in menopause in order to avoid my period.

The battle continued.

They operated on me in January 2014, a ten-hour surgery that left me in bits. But the worse was still to come, because initially it seemed that everything went well, but then suddenly and inexplicably, in the following days, there were complications, resulting in septicemia.

Once again they had to operate on me urgently, 10 days after my last surgery. The doctors did everything to save me.

I awakened extremely tired but with hope. I was surrounded by people who loved me and even Friar Benedetto was there, who would come regularly to visit me. It filled my heart with great joy.

Once I was released from the hospital and after all of the suffering I had endured there, I was able to breathe in some fresh air. Finally, Friar Beningo's secretary called me, giving me an appointment.

I went to the appointment, but to be honest, I was very discouraged and filled with sorrow, given all that had it occurred. I was hopeless.

Friar Benigno received me in the small room situated on the first floor of an old building next to a church. He had me sit in the chair in front of him, where he was seated in the little schoolroom chair, taking notes in his agenda, as I spoke.

After our long conversation I remember he told me, with a beautiful smile: "Have no fear. We'll do this - have faith. From now on I will remember you as December 6" (which was the date in which he wrote my story in this little, old notebook).

Given my delicate state after my surgery, he limited himself to doing some lighter prayers. Then he gave me a date for another appointment.

Subsequently, though, the prayers of exorcism were much more head on, forceful, and violent. He always carried them out in the presence of two medical doctors while my family members helped to restrain me when I became violent.

In one of these encounters, after the initial conversation with Friar Benigno, he had me sit on the little chair. Before he sat down he put on a very long violet stole. Part of this habit was along Rosary with a large crucifix at the end, and on the table he had across and a book of prayers. He sat in front of me and began to pray.

My family members recount the following:

FB: He began to recite the Litany of the Saints with everybody present.

A: Still in silence in the chair.

FB: He began to recite the exorcism in Latin.

A: I began to cry out, swaying in my chair, murmuring and swearing, "what the f… do you want, priest?"

FB: "I want you to leave in the name of Jesus."

A: "No."

FB: "Are you alone?"

A: "No."

FB: "How many are you?"

A: "Many."

FB: "Tell me who you are…. What's your name?"

A: Silence…..

FB: He continued to pray in Latin.

A: I began to writhe about and to scream.

FB: "Tell me your name."

A: "No."

FB: He began to pray a mystery of the Rosary.

A: I became furious and everybody had to hold me down.

A: "F… you, Priest. She's mine."

FB: "She belongs to Jesus."

A: "No…. to me."

FB: "Tell me who you are…" and he continued to pray the Rosary.

A: With a gravelly, cavernous voice, I said, "Asmodeus."

FB: "I order you in the name of Jesus to depart… Jesus orders you."

A: I writhed about, attempting to vomit but nothing came out.

FB: Seeing that I was exhausted, he closed the exorcism. He made me come close to him and told me to repeat: "Lord Jesus, I believe in you; Lord Jesus, I hope you; Lord Jesus, I love you."

A: I said it with great difficulty - but those words say everything.

The following exorcisms seemed harder and more violent, but the most brutal episodes were interior: it became more and more evident that I had lesions within my body. The surgeries left me in a weakened state and I was forced to leave my city in search of other doctors who were equipped to help me find a solution for my problems.

After examining my case, they suggested, unfortunately, two more surgeries. Consequently I returned home quite frightened, evermore filled with anguish and fatigue, but still maintaining a minimum of hope in my heart that things would work out well for me.

Upon my return I recounted everything to Friar Benigno, who continued his exorcisms. That was February, 2015.

I underwent two surgeries in the space of two months and then returned to Friar Benigno to recommence the exorcisms, on the one hand exhausted, but on the other relieved because I thought that finally I would have my problems resolved.

My state of relief did not last long because things took a turn for the worse once again, spontaneously and inexplicably. They found a sort of acute infection within me which put me in bed again with very high fevers. I was once again given a regimen of antibiotics that, inexplicably, brought about no change. Every month I went in and out of hospitals visiting different doctors, but none of them could figure out what I had.

The situation obliged me to cancel some of my appointments with Friar Benigno, and that's when things got really bad. What most scared me was the multiplicity of obstacles between me and friar Benigno. Something or someone was keeping me from receiving more exorcisms.

Once again I ended up in the emergency room with a grave infection that was compromising my kidney. None of the doctors who examined me found the solution, nor could they offer me any hope until there was a small ray of light in my life: one of the doctors took all my paperwork and studied it, returning three days later suggesting another surgery, but not promising anything certain.

I had to undergo a sixth surgery but it was my only hope. And I held onto that hope with the little strength I had left.

I went home living in the expectation of the surgery, but tired of being sick, tired of hospitals, tired of medicines, tired of withdrawals and the seemingly endless CAT scans.

I was attacking my thoughts that day, bringing about within my heart all sorts of sorrow and discouragement. There were so few days when I felt healthy in comparison to the days when I was sick.

When I was a little better I continued to have exorcisms with friar Benigno and they continued to take a lot out of me.

The penultimate exorcism:

As he usually does, Friar Benigno had me sit in a little chair and he, before sitting down came close to me, placing his long stole on me. He still wore his long rosary with the large crucifix at the end and this time he had a cross in one hand and the book of prayer in the other. Thus he began the prayer.

My family members recount the following:

FB: He began to recite the Litany of the Saints with everyone.

A: I started to laugh, getting agitated suddenly. I spat on him and leapt from my chair trying to bite him. A volley of curse words came out of my mouth. "What the f… do you want, priest?"

FB: "I want you to leave in the name of Jesus."

A: "I can't."

FB: "Why can't you?"

A: "He's keeping me here, I have a task."

FB: "Who is keeping you here?"

A: "My Lord."

FB: "Are you alone?"

A: "Yes."

FB: "Tell me who you are. What's your name?"

A: I shouted and said, "Unclean", spitting I'm swearing at everybody present.

FB: "What do you want with her?"

A: "I have to take her away."

FB: "What is your task?"

A: Silence.

FB: "Speak…. I order you in the name of Jesus."

A: "No, he'll punish me."

FB: "Who? Your Lord?"

A: I let out a loud cry and said, "yes."

FB: "Leave her."

A: "I can't…. in a little while, priest."

FB: "In a little while what?"

A: "Leave me alone, priest? What is she to you? Just a little while"

FB: With all of the strengths of his heart he continued to pray. Then he ordered the unclean spirit in the name of Jesus to leave, sprinkling me with holy water.

A: I let out an inhuman "NO!" and fell to the ground.

FB: He called me, "Aurora, look at me. Is that you?"

A: I nodded yes.

FB: "Then repeat together with me: Lord Jesus, I believe in you; Lord Jesus, I hope you; Lord Jesus, I love you."

A: I repeated everything.

I remember that, as I came to, I wept so much, looking around me with fear, hugging from Benigno's leg – I didn't want to let him go. I have the sensation that something was prowling around me and if only I could stay close to the priest I'd be safe.

Friar Benigno calmed me down, saying: "be calm, Aurora, everything is over."

Everybody there thought that this was the definitive deliverance and we all breathed a sigh of relief and joy. Even Friar Benigno thought this was the case, although with some reserve, because the demons, after having manifested, can hide again, leading people to believe that a deliverance has occurred. At the behest, and even under pressure from my family, I decided to go for another exorcism before my surgery, which was slated for November 20, 2015.

There was no way Friar Benigno could know what awaited him, in fact, none of us could have imagined what lay in store for us on November 14, 2015, the appointed day for our exorcism. It was not only the day of my last exorcism, but also the decisive day for the final combat; a day that marked all of our lives, especially mine, forever.

As was the habit, after the initial conversation with friar Benigno, he had me sit on the little chair. Before he sat down he put on a very long violet stole. Part of this habit was along Rosary with a large crucifix at the end, and on the table he had across and a book of prayers. He sat in front of me and began to pray.

The following occurred as my family relates:

FB: With great faith and humility, he began to pray the Litany of the Saints along with everybody.

A: At first I was stiff as a statue, no reactions, immobile, but then I began to laugh, swearing and filling the room with insults.

FB: With great authority he ordered, "Who are you? Tell me your name."

A: I just laughed.

FB: "What do you want with Aurora?"

A: "I want her... She's mine."

FB: "She is a daughter of God, if she's baptized."

A: "No", I screamed.

FB: "How did you enter?"

A: "She called on me."

FB: "She who?"

A: "The knots, priest; you can't undo them."

FB: "Knot's? Jesus can undo them and I command in the name of Jesus that these knots be undone."

A: Tears and suffering... Tears and sufferings, I went crazy.

FB: With great fervor he continued the exorcism in Latin and then commanded, "Tell me your name."

A: Continuing to scream, I said: "Finish up, priest, and shut up. Get lost, leave me alone." Then I spat on him and fell from the chair. His team members, that is the two doctors and my family members, tried to restrain me and hold me still.

FB: With insistence, "I exorcise you, unclean spirit."

A: Writhing, I let out one extended and frightening scream. It seemed that I wouldn't give up and I stared at him intently.

FB: Without giving up, he continued with all of his strength and finally obliged the demon to reveal his name: "Now, tell me who you are…. I command you in the Name of Jesus to tell me who you are."

A: With a very deep, inhuman death rattle, I said: "Satan."

FB: "Leave, Satan. Depart from her in the Name of Jesus."

A: "No, she's mine."

FB: "She belongs to Jesus."

The desperate battle lasted two hours. Friar Benigno knew that Satan was hard to beat, so he canceled all of the following appointments for the day in order to continue this until the end, till Satan eventually left.

Everybody there was worried, weeping and praying. Friar Benigno continued with his endless Rosaries.

And then a very intense dialogue ensued:

A: Up against the wall and standing in front of him, I said: "So here we are, priest. Good and evil." Meanwhile everyone tried to restrain me on account of my superhuman strength.

FB: He prohibited Satan from interfering with the surgery.

A: "No, priest, that's exactly how I will bring her with me. Blood, she will lose so much blood."

FB: "Jesus Christ is stronger than you."

A: "He's dead."

FB: "Silence, Jesus Christ has triumphed over death and he has defeated you."

A: "I know why you want her."

FB: "Oh yeah?"

A: "Because she is a good soul."

FB: "Leave her body, I command you in Jesus Christ."

A: I fell my knees, retching. "Are you done, priest?"

FB: "Leave her in the Name of Jesus."

A: I spat on him, trying to bite him, screaming, "No" as Friar Benigno sprinkled me with holy water. Falling prostrate, I tried to wiggle away from him, all the while screaming accusations and obscenities. Then I said, "Get lost, priest. You again. Why do I always have to deal with you? I can't stand you. You have an angel close to you who protects you."

FB: "Depart. You know I'm willing to be here this evening and all of tomorrow, so now I'll say another mystery of the Rosary."

A: "No!" I was thrown up against the wall in cruciform, shouting: "IIIIIIIIIIIIIII... am god!"

FB: "So are you leaving?"

A: I nodded my head as if to say yes. But it was a deception. Satan was lying.

FB: He brought me close to him to make me repeat: " Lord Jesus, I believe in you; Lord Jesus, I hope you; Lord Jesus, I love you."

A: I didn't repeat anything, but rather came close to him to break Rosary that I hated so much.

FB: Once again he asked if I come back to myself and he told me to repeat the words, "Lord Jesus, I believe in you; Lord Jesus, I hope you; Lord Jesus, I love you."

A: I only said, "I believe in you," without adding "Lord Jesus".

FB: he understood that I was not speaking to Jesus and so we continued another mystery of the Rosary.

A: I was at the end of my rope. I crawled on the ground as Friar Benigno placed the cross on my forehead, and I let out a cry of defeat. Then, suddenly, while everybody was praying, Friar Benigno asked everybody to be silent.

A: I had fainted and fallen to the ground. Suddenly, I begin to recite a beautiful prayer. It was soft and sweet, like a voice from heaven. I was praying to the Blessed Virgin Mary

FB: "That's it, she's praying to the Virgin Mary."

After three hours of exorcism we all wept for joy.

I woke up as if from a profound sleep and, for the first time, felt fine. I remember my first words: "The Blessed Virgin Mary is so beautiful. I saw her." As I said this I could see the faces of everyone around me streaming tears, tears of joy, because what happen was truly a miracle.

Everyone asked how she was.

I saw her light, felt her immense mercy. With her intercession she saved me and freed me from the serpent who was destroying my life and wanted to take me with him.

The battle was so hard, but in the end Jesus Christ triumphed.

Friar Benigno approached me, joking: "Now we can make up, we've fought enough" and I let loose a cry of freedom.

I was finally free and had my life back. I remember feeling like I was born again, but to a new life, this time with extraordinary peace in my heart.

The surgery on November 20 went very well and the problem that should have left me an invalid for the rest of my life was miraculously resolved.

Even in subsequent sessions of exorcism with Friar Benigno everything went well: there were no more reactions as in past sessions, and I didn't enter into a trance. Returning home after the exorcisms I not only remembered everything, but was also relieved of all of the pains in my body, the contortions in my face, the discouragement and everything else that filled my life with anguish. I no longer had to stay in bed with such horrible pain in my bones.

Friar Benigno warned me that having been possessed and delivered is an experience can return, because the demons hang around to tempt the person to sin. After having been delivered it would be a great victory for them for someone to fall into a mortal sin and that could open the door, bringing about their return. And if that were the case it would be more difficult to be delivered. Consequently, he exhorted me to cultivate a deep friendship with the Lord and to receive the sacraments frequently: confession and Eucharist, since those are the greatest protections against the attacks of the devil, something I do with great pleasure.

Today, finally, I live in peace, and evil, the Evil One, no longer has a place in my life. All of those illnesses that made me suffer so much disappeared with my deliverance. All of those terrible abdominal pains, with their frequent hemorrhages and vomiting that kept me in bed for so long, disappeared.

The inexplicable and extreme alterations of weight gain and loss have also disappeared, as have the spontaneous kidney blockages.

My endometriosis – and all that it brought with it – disappeared.

I no longer have the septicemia. In fact, all of those inexplicable illnesses and fatigues that I endured before my deliverance have come to a halt. Now my health is stable.

The episodes of rage that occurred in my house when I was alone, with all of the invective directed towards myself and the self-harm, remain in the past.

The whispering voice inciting me to beat myself and take my life has been reduced to silence.

All of this is thanks to the gift of exorcism that Jesus has given to his Church.

At last I can sleep well, enjoying a deep sleep without the nightmares that used to interrupt my every night. The violent physical attacks and the sexual assaults I had to endure are no more.

Ever since my deliverance I can participate in Mass without crying or entering into a crisis, without experiencing that ferocious hatred and violence towards everyone, especially towards the priest who offers Mass. Every week I go to Mass and experience great joy, comfort and, above all consolation when I receive the Eucharist.

Today, after my deliverance, I feel the need to be close to God and I go to confession every week, praying my Rosary every day.

At last the Sacred Rota granted the degree of nullity of marriage, and along with that I was granted a civil nullification, which my lawyer told me it would be very difficult to obtain because of certain problems that presented themselves during the process. What is impossible for man is possible for God.

Suddenly, if not to say miraculously, I was healed of all of the links from my past.

Wearing the miraculous medal on the Rosary around my neck I feel protected by the company of the Blessed Virgin Mary.

I would like to end saying that Good and Evil truly exist and that their fight reaches to the very roots of our dark times. I have known Evil, even if I never saw his face. I've experienced such attacks in my own flesh, leaving me to weep over being made the plaything of his perverse games. I felt his presence in my life as well as his insidious blows. Darkness, sorrow, and anguish all took up residence in my heart for a long time. The Evil One wanted me, he wanted my soul, my life; but the infinite love of God saved me because God does not abandon his children. He chose to die for us rather than live without us. And through the intercession of His merciful Mother, the Blessed Virgin Mary, he saved me, showing me, little by little, the way towards the light. The battle was extremely difficult but Jesus triumphed.

For good to overcome evil we have to pray very much. And so today, I would ask anyone who is going through a difficult period, thinking that there is no exit, to pray and believe with all one's heart, because whatever the nature of your dark tunnel, and however long it may seem, for those who truly believe, there is light.

Marcella: from possession to deliverance with her faithful husband at her side

After 11 years of courtship, we were finally married in August 2005. My husband Giuseppe is a land surveyor.

While we were going out, his business prowess grew from day to day, and he built a financial empire made up of real estate, an amusement park, and other facilities that were the envy of many. In our part of the country my husband and his business were the frequent topic of discussion. During that time I matriculated in university. After graduating with a degree in architecture with honors, getting married, and going on our honeymoon, I went into business with him.

Before our marriage, everything seemed to go very well for us. Our life was a fairytale, just as I always dreamed it ought to be - something I had lots of time to do that during 11 years of courtship! We lived in a beautiful house with every comfort.

We invited many people to our wedding. Many of the guests hired security to watch over their houses while they were at the wedding since practically everybody from our small town was there, turning it into a ghost town.

Things continued to go splendidly for us open until the baptism of our second daughter, Carla. Since we had business matters all over Sicily – with over $25 million dollars invested - my husband was obliged to travel very much, overseeing more than 100 employees. We purchased an apartment building, turning it into an office building with eight departments spread out over two floors.

Everyone had their task: my brother-in-law and I oversaw the technical part; my sister-in-law worked on contracts (public and private); while my husband oversaw the administration and personnel, and others worked in finances.

We baptized our baby in September 2008.

On November 4, 2008, my husband appeared in all of the newspapers with headlines reading: "Mafia Infiltration Sees Firm's Public Contracts Revoked."

Thus began Giuseppe's seemingly endless trips to and from the banks who had lost all their trust in us, demanding investigations for every check, and submitting every move we made to its security department. Everyone whom we thought to be a friend of my husband distanced himself from us to avoid problems.

A similar coming and going of lawyers began, first administrative and then criminal, all incurring substantial costs. Eventually, in order to pay the legal fees for the many hearings at the regional administrative court, we had to sell everything: apartments, our car, and even my jewelry. The cases were always dismissed "for lack of evidence."

Our lawyer, one of the best criminal law attorneys in Palermo, a devout Catholic, took our situation to heart. He was pulling his hair out because he couldn't figure out what the local and state government officials wanted. It reached such a point that he confessed to Giuseppe, "I feel like I don't even know how to do my job anymore – I know how to get falsely accused people off of murder charges, but I'm at a loss in your case. In all my years as a lawyer, I've never seen anything like this."

In fact, the justice department of Palermo transferred the case to Trapani. Trapani, in their turn, remitted it to the justice department of Marsala. And all of this without any explanation.

When we finally arrived at the Justice Department of Marsala, they told us that they had lost all of the documentation on the matter. After eight months they contacted us telling us that they had found the files in a seldom-used room, lost in a stack of documents awaiting to be archived.

Consequently, we would be judged in Marsala (two hours away), when all along, if something had to be decided, it should have been in Palermo.

Under all of this stress my husband went from 175 pounds to 245 pounds. The constant tension made him physically ill, bringing him to vomit up blood every morning, and becoming quite taciturn. He didn't want to speak with anyone. So as not to make a scene, he would hide out in the bedroom, curled up in a ball weeping. I could hear him mumbling, "Why me? What did I do to deserve this?"

After a year of this suffering, my husband and his mother visited a monastery where an exorcist worked, but the doors were locked. There was a note saying that the priest was quite ill and was not able to attend to the afflicted. Strangely enough, a woman saw them reading the note and suggested that they visit another priest in Caltanisetta. He too was an exorcist.

My husband came home delighted with this new information. I, on the other hand, strangely was upset. In fact, I told him, "All the way to Caltanisetta? That's too far!" On the other hand, I was happy to see him finally smile.

We left our house for Caltanisetta and I didn't say a word on the whole trip there. After driving around town a little while, we finally found the church, a small parish in the middle of the city. Once we arrived at the front door, I told my husband: "You go in, I'll wait outside." He looked at me and said, "What? After all of that trip you want to stay outside?" He noticed a sudden change in my expression.

Giuseppe:

Not only did my wife's expression change drastically, she couldn't even breathe. She became paralyzed and didn't want any of us to touch her. Turning furiously to me I could see how her face had become so ugly. I took her by force and dragged her into the church. I had use all of my strength to restrain her because she was manifesting wildly and didn't want to come into the church. Her head was whipping around and her entire body began to convulse and contort.

In that moment the exorcist arrived, accompanied by a man in a wheelchair. At the sight of the priest she began to gasp, then she began spitting on him, saying all sorts of nasty things, laughing, crying, and all along foam was coming out of her mouth. It was horrible.

When the priest commanded during the exorcism: "In the Name of Jesus, tell me your name," my wife went into a trance and began to say a series of names with a very strange voice that sounded like that of an old woman: "Asmodeus, Beelzebub, Beliz," and other names I don't remember. He also said that there was an entire legion of demons in her.

Marcella:

On the way back home my husband didn't say a word about what happened in the little room of the church. And I couldn't remember anything.

We began to go to Caltanisetta every week. My husband stopped worrying about all of the legal problems, and in fact, he didn't really even care about them anymore. All he thought about was helping me to get better, accompanying me in my exorcisms. Over the space of the year and a half I had exorcisms two days a week.

The day before our trial at Marsala, the exorcist's secretary called us saying that he wanted to speak with us. My husband and I met in Palermo and went together to Caltanisetta. I got in his car and after 200 yards the car stalled in the middle of an intersection right in the center of Palermo.

The car was a goner. We were able to get some help and we left the heap with someone we knew. Giuseppe called his brother who brought us one of his cars, an off-road vehicle. As we drove to Caltanisetta we met a furious storm whose wind and rain made driving quite difficult.

As soon as we got out of Palermo and came to Casteldaccia we were stopped by a public transport road crew who sent us on a detour all the way back towards Palermo because the road was out on account of a landslide. My husband, always stubborn, looked at me saying, "that's why we have an off-road. Don't worry, we'll make it. Father was the one who called us, so the Lord will bless us."

As soon as we got to Caltanisetta, the car began to make strange sounds, the steering wheel was shaking, we had a flat. The tire was in strips but my husband continued to drive. We made it to the church on wheel rims. Father smiled at us and said, "A little trouble getting here?"

Giuseppe:

The exorcist began his prayer of exorcism. When he sprinkled the holy water on my wife, she began to scream as if she were being whipped. I was holding her down in a chair that ended up in bits on the floor. I could hardly hold it still given the strength of the thing within her. The priest picked up his phone and called for help from a nun in the convent asking her to pray for my wife. The exorcism prayer last around 40 minutes. My wife was a mess at the end, but I think I was worse off. I just wept. At that time the nun called and said, "you have an ugly, twisted object in your house that was cursed by a witch." She said she saw something about the staircase. And then she told us to read a verse from the Bible, which I don't remember anymore.

Marcella:

One day, while we were in Caltanisetta, awaiting our turn for exorcism, we met a couple from Palermo. They told us about another exorcist in Palermo, a French Franciscan friar who worked in the monastery near Saint Isidore Baida, a section of the town. His name was Friar Benedetto.

Giuseppe:

We made an appointment with him and as this friar began to say the exorcism prayer in French, my wife, who entered into a trance, began to respond to him in French, a language she had never learned. And then she began to manifest as she had in Caltanisetta.

Marcella:

We were able to successfully address the legal situation, but things continued to go poorly for us. It seemed that the more we worked, the more we lost money. My husband, who is normally gregarious and joking, lost his smile. Nonetheless, aware of the presence of the Evil One within me, he exhibited so much strength and an iron will. He never abandoned me for an instant during those seven years of possession. He was humiliated, he wept, but never gave up. He also started to seek the help of other exorcists.

We continued to go to Caltanisetta and Palermo for exorcisms but could find no deliverance. Finally, the French exorcist in Palermo was transferred. He told me that I would have to meet Friar Benigno, who was taking his place.

We went to meet him but were greeted by one of his team members at the Listening Center. We began to tell our story and this person understood quite quickly that this was an actual case that would require Friar Benigno. But then this person asked what diocese we lived in. As soon as we said that we did not live in the confines of the Diocese of Palermo, and that in fact, we had seen other exorcists, he told us that it would not be possible for us to be received by Friar Benigno, since he was already overwhelmed with the amount of cases he had.

My husband asked Friar Benigno to consider taking us on, even though we were not from his diocese, since we had such need of his help. The person we had met earlier encouraged Friar Benigno to take us on, at which point he made an appointment for us.

FB:

In the initial dialogue I came to understand that, among other things, Marcella had a difficult time going to Mass and it was almost impossible for her to receive the Eucharist. After Communion she had terrible pain in her back and her tongue was as if on fire.

She had a groundless hatred towards her husband and tried to avoid sexual relations with him. When they did in fact have relations, she experienced horrible pain in her genital area and would always vomit after each conjugal act. This began in the year 2008. She had the sensation of being observed or followed and then during the night, she would experience some sexual disturbances that increased to the point of penetration. She noted a degree of improvement thanks to the prayers that had been done.

The phenomenon of sexual abuse by an unseen being is a strange one, indeed. I first heard about it from an African exorcist in the year 2000 at the gathering of the *International Association of Exorcists*. He said that in his country those demons were called *night husbands* – invisible entities that sexually abused women even unto sexual relations. Since I come from the world of philosophy I found this testimony quite strange, thinking within myself, "This exorcist is crazy!" He went on to tell us that with exorcism this phenomena eventually disappears.

Returning to Palermo and beginning to carry out my ministry as an exorcist, I discovered that this phenomenon actually does take place even in our country. But I noticed a constant amongst all of these cases: when it happened to married women it was always accompanied by a strong aversion towards their husbands, culminating in hatred and the refusal to have conjugal relations. Further, those that eventually did have conjugal relations with her husbands ended up vomiting after each conjugal act, and experienced horrible pain in the genitals.

It was always the same with these women: as soon as I began the prayer of exorcism, they would enter into a trance and the new personality would emerge that reacted strongly to my prayers. But then when I would address the demon with the name Asmodeus as found in the Book of Tobit, he would react in fury. And with exorcisms these phenomena would diminish and eventually disappear in all every aspect: the vomiting, the pain, the baseless hatred towards their spouses, and they would return to life as before. This happened in cases of possession and oppression. Obviously, it is not the case that Asmodeus truly has sexual relations with women, since he is an angel, a spiritual being is incapable of something of that sort. On the other hand, he has the ability to bring about in the woman, through oppression, all of the typical sensations of sexual relations.

This brings up a question: how is it that only exorcists run into these cases, while other priests have never heard of it? I suppose the reason would be that it is quite difficult already for women to speak about things of this nature. And to bring it up with the priest, she runs the risk of being treated as abnormal or out of her mind, being sent to see a psychiatrist to take care of her problem. All of this just adds to the burden. Women seem to prefer to only speak about things of this nature with an exorcist in hopes that he may understand her.

As soon as I began the exorcism Marcella entered into a trance. There were the typical reactions that I see in possessed people. When I gave him the command in Latin to tell me his name, he said, "Asmodeus," I then asked him in Italian if he was alone and he responded that there was a whole Legion. When she came out of the trance she could remember nothing that had occurred.

I performed the first exorcism on September 11, 2014. The last one, the one in which I realized that her deliverance was definitive, was on May 2, 2015, after two days of people visiting our church praying the Rosary for the deliverance of the people who came to me to receive exorcisms. During that exorcism there was no reaction, nor were there any in successive exorcisms: all of the signs of definitive deliverance were evident.

Giuseppe:

The first encounter with Friar Benigno, after having told him our story, began with him doing the initial prayers, after which my wife began to feel sick, cold, trembling. Then she told Friar Benigno to mind his own business and go about his things. When he asked in the name of God who it was that was speaking to him, the response was: "Asmodeus." He said that he was the leader of a legion of demons and that he had been entrusted with the mission to carry out. When Friar Benigno asked what the nature of the task was, he said: "I have to destroy their work, and their marriage, and then kill her husband." And then turning to Friar Benigno: "Mind your own business." And then, returning to me, said: "And you, you better stop running around looking for exorcists everywhere. I'll ruin you. I want to see you dead."

Friar Benigno responded: "You are nobody and you will harm no one." To which the demon replied, "Tonight I'll come to you and I'll show you what I'm capable of doing."

"Sure, come along," said Friar Benigno, "you can pray the Rosary with me."

"Stuff it. You better show me some respect," was his response.

"My respect is for God, the Blessed Virgin Mary, the Angels and the Saints, and of course, none for you."

He then stared him in the eyes and said, "Remember well that God despises nothing that he has created." He was referring to the verse *For you love all things that are and loathe nothing that you have made; for what you hated, you would not have fashioned* (Wisdom 11:24). In other words, if God does not despise anything that he has created, then you must not despise me because I am part of his creation. If God does not despise me, it means that He respects me. And if God respects me, then you ought to give me respect as well.

Marcella:

After that exorcism was done, I went home and, as usual, could remember nothing that had happened. The only difference this time was that I felt more peace, freer, calmer.

That was November, 2014. A friend of mine was transferred to Fano for work reasons and she invited us to spend the weekend with her. I was upset because I was sure that my husband given our circumstances would surely say no. Surprisingly he said yes and immediately bought our plane tickets and we took off.

Arriving in Fano we decided to go for a walk. As we were walking we stopped in front of the bookstore. My daughter asked if we could buy a book of children's stories for her. I went in search for books of that sort while my husband looked for other ones. He brought to the checkout two books, *My Possession* by Francesco Vaiasuso and *Against Satan* by Father Matteo La Grua. I asked him why he bought those books but he gave me no answer. He put the books in the bag and we continued our walk. As soon as we got to the hotel he didn't even notice the time because he wanted to read the books. He stayed up until 3 AM reading one of those books until finally I said to him, "Giueseppe, come on, turn out the light, it's late."

In the morning he felt sick, in lots of pain, with a sore right side, and severe nausea. He told me that he and had a horrible nightmare that seemed so real: he had a dream in which he had sexual relations with a faceless, hooded person. He was then tied up and beaten.

The next night he continued reading and had the same nightmare. He was an insistent on continuing to read and finally finished the book on the third night. He was a mess but victorious.

Returning home, he said: "Marcella, that book was written by a young man from Alcamo who went through hell. He was actually possessed by 27 legions of demons. You only have one. We can do this."

He contacted Francesco Vaiasuso, who responded to his email and gave him an appointment for Tuesday in Alcamo at 8:30 in a prayer meeting.

That was November 25, 2014. We took off for Alcamo. Since my husband didn't know the place, he put the address in the GPS. I was disgusted and came up with 2000 excuses: "Who will I leave the children with?" To which he said, "Don't worry, I invited your parents to our house and they'll take care of them." And then I said, "we have a 5 AM flight for Rome tomorrow, it's too early." And he said," don't worry, five hours are enough to sleep." Fine, it's useless to argue with him.

Once we arrived at Alcamo, we came to a roundabout but the GPS said, "You've arrived at your destination." My husband checked the GPS and the address was still the same. We tried the same with the cell phone map and had the same results. When we tried using our tablet, it too told us that we had arrived.

Seeing him in such a desperate state, I told him that I thought I knew the road and I guided him there. We came to a church with an enormous glass door. As soon as the car stopped, he jumped out and ran ahead without even telling me what were going to do. As he entered the church he looked back and said, "Look, do you see that guy? That has to be Francesco." I told him, "That's not Francesco." He asked. It wasn't Francesco. They told us that we find him up in front.

Finally, we came to where Francesco was. We took a seat. "Giuseppe," I said, "I bet the kids are upset." I then began checking my phone to see if my mother had called. I also reminded him that I had an exposition in Rome the next day. It was like talking to a wall. My husband was very attentive while I, on the other hand, was bored and became cranky just being in that room seeing all of those happy people praying and singing. But what most made me angry was the presence of Francesco.

Immediately after the prayer meeting, my husband made a beeline for Francesco. I followed behind. I began to feel sick and couldn't even look at him. Francesco came to me and gave me a hug, saying, "I was waiting for you." And then came the cold shower: "You have to forgive your mother-in-law." I looked at him: "No, I can't forgive her and I'm happy that she's suffering." My husband was reduced to silence.

The truth is that before my marriage, I never had an argument with my mother-in-law and our relationship was beautiful. She treated me as if I were her daughter. But one fine day, after the marriage and when I just had my second daughter, the work problems began. With that, her attitude towards me changed. She seemed to have a sort of jealousy of me and couldn't stand me anymore. And from that moment, on my own behavior towards her changed as well.

Francesco kept on telling me, "You have to forgive her if you want to be delivered."

And then at a certain moment I don't know what penetrated my heart. Suddenly tremendous joy filled me. Crying and hugging Francesco, I said, "Yes, I do forgive her." I went to confession to a certain Father Giuseppe who was with the prayer group. Francesco told me that 25 November was the day of my true deliverance. The truth of the matter is that it wasn't just yet.

On November 27 we had an appointment with Friar Benigno. When we got there, my husband took out of his pocket a crucifix that he used to have hanging in his car, as if it were his guardian angel. It was an ugly thing, all dented and broken, as if it had received many hammer blows, dirty and crooked. That crucifix belonged to his mother who said that she received it from an exorcist. My husband put it in his office, hanging it behind the main entrance around the end of October, 2008, to ward off any envy and protect the workplace.

at the moment that the crucifix was placed on the table, I turned to my husband and told him to put it back. Friar Benigno asked at that moment if that's what was bothering me. "Yes," I responded. He told me to look at another crucifix, the one that he had and, looking at it, I noticed that it didn't bother me. I mentioned this to Friar Benigno. With that he told me that the crucifix had to be destroyed. As soon as he picked it up to put it in the bag, I entered into a trance.

FB: But did that crucifix really come from an exorcist?

Marcella: my husband always told me that it had been given to him by his mother and that she had received it from an exorcist. After my deliverance I investigated its origins. Upon telling my mother-in-law everything that had happened with the crucifix during the exorcism, she said that, in fact, she didn't remember where it came from.

A little background: my husband and I both remembered at the same time what had been told to us at Caltanisetta: that we had something ugly in the house, a twisted object upon which a curse had been placed. We never thought it could be the crucifix.

One day, taking it in my hands, I saw the demon who had taken power over me and did not want to let me go. I understood that it was bound to that object which had been identified when we were in Caltanisetta. So I decided to bring it to Friar Benigno.

Giuseppe: That new personality who emerged in my wife when Friar Benigno took the crucifix and put it in the bag to destroy it, flung himself at me, challenging me: "Now you've got to decide. You have to tell me which of the two I will take, your mother or your wife." Then he added, "And you better stop running around looking for help from people and talking to them. I'm at the point of destroying you. I have to fulfill my mission. I've been paid and one of them has to die."

Immediately Friar Benigno intervened, saying: "Neither of the two is going to die."

At that point, the new personality that had emerged in my wife began to scream: "Why do you have the courage to forgive your mother-in-law, to confess your sins, and even pray the Rosary…. How could you manage to forgive, after everything you've been through?" And then, with the desperation, he said, "I'm going now, leaving," and immediately after that came the deliverance, if only for little while.

Marcella: When we left I told my husband, "Call your mother. I'm worried about her." He phoned her but there was no response. He then tried his father, the same thing.

After a half hour his father called back saying they couldn't pick up because something strange happened to his wife: everything was fine and then suddenly she began to wet herself, urinating without ceasing. All of this happened in the moment in which the demon desperately cried out, "I'm leaving."

From that day onwards my family began to get better and gradually return to the normalcy we enjoyed before. After two years we finally won a public contract and with that money were able to put up Christmas decorations and invite people to our house.

FB: In the exorcism of December 12, 2014, during the preliminary interview, Marcella remarked to me that after the preceding exorcism, she vomited the whole way home. She also told me that since the last session she had been feeling fine, calm, with a clear mind - and no evil thoughts. In the days afterwards, on the other hand, she had a burning sensation on her tongue that lasted for two hours after Communion. She arrived limping.

Marcella: my deliverance did not happen on December 12, 2014, but rather just before the exorcism on May 2, 2015. When I returned to Friar Benigno for my usual exorcism, I immediately lost control of myself. But unlike other times, remained conscious. Suddenly I felt as if a dagger had penetrated my abdomen and I felt as if somebody had cut my bellybutton open.

As soon as the dagger was taken out, I could breathe again and saw an ugly figure leave me. From that moment onwards, all of my disturbances ceased:

- I no longer had difficulty attending Mass or receiving Communion.
- Strong pains in my back came to an end.
- Before, I would always wake up in the morning as if I had a body on top of me and I couldn't get out of bed. Ever since my deliverance I no longer experience this. I spend my days and nights in peace, and sleep the whole night through.
- I no longer experience groundless hatred towards my husband for the aversion to conjugal relations with him. And when we have relations I no longer experience all of the horrible pains in my genitals. Matrimonial relations no longer produce nausea and vomiting.
- Now I don't feel like somebody is watching me or following me. No more sexual assaults by an invisible figure.
- My mind, which had become quite cloudy, is now clear and I can reflect with calm, carrying out my work and other tasks without problems. Before, I needed everything explained to me multiple times and I still could not understand what was supposed to be done. I was also making all sorts of errors, signing contracts with people who had no credit, etc.
- My husband and I have rediscovered a certain empathy, our old sense of teamwork which made us fall in love

with each other. Certainly we drew from it in all of these years in which our love was tested; it's what kept us together during the difficult years of my possession.

In the exorcism of May 2, 2015, Friar Benigno was able to verify that the definitive deliverance had occurred: there were no reactions, I remained conscious and I could participate actively in all of the prayers.

Returning several times more to receive his prayers I continued to remain lucid and I experienced no disturbances.

I want to thank the Lord for the gift of the deliverance he has granted me. I think my heavenly Mother who allowed me to experience the joy of being delivered in her month of May. I want to thank my husband as well. He stood by me in all of my trials.

Marianna: from a life of sin to the Kingdom of Light

So much drama touches the lives of so many people, especially when they live the disorder of sin, a life far from the Gospel. Such a context, naturally, leaves all sorts of windows and doors open to the devil's extraordinary action. Once he enters, he turns their lives upside down. Such is the case of Marianna.

Reading her testimony, we will shortly, along with her, render the Lord proper praise for his action in her life. Today she is truly reborn. From a life of sin that included living with somebody who was not her spouse and cultivating hatred, she arrived at the kingdom of light and friendship with God. Since she and her consort had a child together, they had to remain together for the good of the child, but committed to live in chastity in preparation for their sacramental marriage.

Beyond the remission of her sins, the Lord also granted her the grace of deliverance from a diabolical possession that had brought so much suffering in its wake, as well as a diabolical infestation that besieged her house. Finally, Marianna is able to smile, and that is thanks to the work of grace brought about by the Lord through the sacrament of reconciliation and the sacramental of exorcism.

Marianna:

I give to the Lord Jesus Christ all my gratitude, praise, all the glory to my Savior for the good he is done for me. Today I offer all of my sufferings to Him in hopes that others, too, may be delivered from the grip of the Evil One.

My name is Marianna, I'm 20 years old and the mother of a beautiful four-year-old boy whom I love more than my own life. From a very early age I suffered all sorts of trials. I do not know what it is to be loved by a mother, much less by a father. The concept of being a loved child is foreign to me, retaining no joyful memories of my childhood. The only memories I have of my parents bring me profound sorrow. And those memories are quite vivid.

I was four when my mother died in a car accident. My father, a violent man infected with AIDS, and now terminal, contracted the illness after having sexual relations with a prostitute, in an extra-marital affair.

I lived in the house in a tiny town in the Province of Trapani with my parents, the same house in which my father's relatives live today, while my mother's side, although in the Province of Agrigento, are not far from them.

During the whole time I was under the same roof as my parents, I have no recollection of any particular attention or manifestations of affection. I spent my days, for the most part, alone making up games with the few objects at my disposal in the house: two plastic horses that were a gift for my maternal grandmother named Giuseppina (Josephine).

I remember one day, as I played with the two horses in the kitchen, the door to the pantry opened by itself. I was curious and entered in, only to see the figure of a little girl about seven years old, dressed in a white dress and hair in braids. The only thing she said was that she was named "Gloria."

This little girl became my only playmate with whom I could speak. Until the period immediately before I met Friar Beningo, she was always at my side in my bedroom, often stroking my head.

One time, when I was still quite young, even my mother saw her and let out a scream, saying that she should never bother me again and ought leave me in peace.

I'm unsure how much time passed, but after that episode my mother suffered her inexplicable car accident, which put an end to her life, crushed between a car and the tree. "Your mother is dead. Don't cry," were the words my father used to inform me of my mother's passing. At the time I was at my maternal grandmother's house, Giuseppina. At a loss and filled with despair, I threw my arms around her neck, weeping.

My father decided to use his widowed state to hook up an old flame, who was also alone, although she had her children with whom she still lives.

If my father never really loved me before, this new situation made his decision to distance himself from me definitive, because his new companion couldn't stand me and didn't want me living with my father.

Consequently, I was dropped off at the house of my paternal grandmother, Teresa. In spite of all of this, my filial instinct made me want to visit my father and his companion in his house, overall it was always the cause of great suffering: frequent slaps and punches and getting the belt for the most minor infractions.

Those visits became a nightmare for me. My father would wait until my arrival to begin having sex with his companion so that I would find them in that state. Sometimes they would lock me in the closet and I would manage to escape only to find them in the act.

These experiences brought about such fury and hatred against both of them, something I vented by enclosing myself in the closet, turning into a victim of my own self-harm: hitting and biting myself.

Beyond the beatings my father meted out according to his own code of justice, my paternal grandmother Teresa would often accuse me of bad behavior and increase the blows. She would warn me that I had better not say anything about what I had seen or experienced to my grandmother Giuseppina, who often came to visit me from Agrigento. She often came to visit me at school, and brought me food because she knew I was malnourished. She also looked after my personal hygiene since nobody gave me a bath at home.

Left to myself, I was often on the street, eating little and not washing myself for days on end. In certain times – especially in the summer – I was abandoned in the street for days, sleeping in drainage pipes. Of course, I was at the mercy of anyone who might find me.

While at my grandmother Teresa's house, some of my father's relatives spoke about my grandfather who had died hogtied, with his hands, feet, and neck bound together behind his back. They said that he was a practitioner of the occult, having cursed many people, bringing untold suffering on entire families, leaving them destitute, and even using death curses.

One of my uncles recounted how my grandfather had been possessed by Asmodeus, among other spirits. My grandfather died while I was still in my mother's womb and, since I was the first feminine grandchild, I was to be possessed by these same spirits.

This horrible secret was hidden from grandmother Teresa who, even today, continues to practice occultism. I remember how she initiated me into these rituals as if it were a game while I was still small.

One time, when I was together with my cousin named Agatha, she got a live mouse and placed it on a plate. Then, covering it with a cup, she submerged it in boiling water which was on the stove next to us. During the ritual and at her command, she made us pronounce a ritual in the form of a song, while the mouse squealed and frantically tried to escape from the pot.

I remember a rag doll that my grandmother Teresa gave me along with some pins. She told me the formula to repeat every time that I stuck one of the pins in a particular section of the doll: the neck, the stomach, the head. I was supposed to carry out this ritual, pronouncing the names of my maternal grandmother Giuseppina and my uncle Rosario, brother of my deceased mother.

One day my uncle Rosario saw me playing with doll and he took it and he threw it in the furnace, burning it. That was when all of my grandmother Giuseppina's illnesses were cleared up. And that was when Rosario's began. He had always enjoyed excellent health but suddenly he developed kidney problems and even today is on dialysis three days a week.

Finally the day came when the children's health and welfare department notified my father that he was losing custody of me after numerous complaints from social workers and police: abuse, negligence, and even the nose he broke when he punched me in the face did not escape their notice.

With that, at the age of 10, I was entrusted to my grandmother Giueseppina and went to live in Agrigento.

While there, I tried forget about my past, but unfortunately the regime imposed upon me by the children's health and welfare department obliged me to undergo a course of reeducation and reintegration through the interventions of social workers and child psychologists who kept on bringing up the past.

In spite of the affection I experienced from my mom's relatives and my grandmother Giuseppina in particular, as the years passed, from deep within me a rabid hatred grew up against everyone else who was loved. For example, my cousin Andrew was doted over and loved by his own parents. In him I saw everything my parents refused me.

A sense of rebellion welled up within me. I hated God because I held him responsible for everything that had happened, especially for having taking my mother in that accident. And so I cursed the day in which I was born and my only prayer to God was that he would take my life.

As all children of my age, I began to go to church, to catechism, and prepare for my First Communion. This changed nothing in me, much to the contrary: an uncontrollable ferocity boiled within me. Whenever I could not get what I wanted, I would commit all sorts of violent acts, so much so that grandmother Giuseppina was the one who really paid the consequences. I even attacked her with fists and feet.

But not only were the others the object of my violent attacks – I did lots of harm to myself as well. In fact this latter behavior worked as a way of getting attention for myself, because I was convinced but I was not loved or even taken into account.

When the day of my First Holy Communion came, I was delighted because I thought that with it everything would change and I, like all of the other children, would somehow return home from church to a happy family, with a mother and father. But, of course, it was all a fantasy.

When I was 15 years, old I met Cyrus and we began to live together, although he would only become my husband on September 3, 2015. In him I found someone to fill the void of love that I always experienced, so much so that I left home to live with him and soon was pregnant. The life of wife and mother was not without its difficulties.

As soon as I realized that I was pregnant with the child, I thought of him just as my parents used to think of me. I kept this sentiment to myself, never showing it. Several times I tried to abort the child with my own methods, punching my stomach, sniffing bleach and gasoline.

One night I had a dream of my mother holding my son and her arms. I awakened with my hand on my womb and there immediately welled up within me the maternal instinct that engendered an unconditional love for my son who was about to be born.

Today I thank God for this beautiful gift that He has given me and I thank him even more because He was the one who protected him. It was through my son that God's plan for my conversion and salvation began to come about.

We're now in April 2013. My son was three years old. It was Easter Sunday and I was at my grandmother Giuseppina's house, with whom we three lived. While I was hurriedly preparing myself to go to my mother-in-law's house, brushing my hair in a mirror in the bedroom, I was aware of the presence of somebody behind me who was blowing on my hair so much so that it came unbrushed. Then a shadowy figure quickly crossed the room.

I didn't give much importance to the episode and convinced myself that it was all in my head.

In June of that same year my disturbances began. I was beaten during the night, bitten, had my hair pulled out, and was choked. In the kitchen cupboards and the drawers opened and violently slammed closed on their own.

Beginning in August 2014 every night I would be stripped naked and have the sensation of being bound and sexually abused. In the morning I would wake up with tremendous pain covered with bruises in scratches and bite marks all over my body. During that time I had a recurring vision: I saw a person whom, in reality, I only knew by sight, standing in front of the rectory of the church of St. Anastasius. When the door would open I would ask him for help but he couldn't see me.

While visiting my partner's uncle in the month of September, he looked at me and said, "Marianna, you look like a vampire. Don't you sleep at night?"

Perhaps it was owing to all of the stress that I was undergoing or the exhaustion of looking for help to relieve me of all of the violence I was suffering, but I stopped having my period. I told him everything that was happening to me each night. This was the first that my partner was aware of what I was undergoing since he's such a deep sleeper. As I spoke about it I began to manifest: my legs were beaten and covered with bruises, while my abdomen was bitten, showing bite marks. My uncle, quite frightened from seeing all of my suffering and hearing my screams, implored Jesus' help.

Meanwhile my father-in-law came in as soon he was as he was called. As he held me down by my arms a table right next to us that no one had touched flew up into the air violently and smashed on the ground. After a little while I came to and I could see that my father-in-law's arm was bleeding. I'm not sure if I bit him or not. Probably.

That evening, returning home, all of the same disturbances repeated themselves but this time more violently. I was abused the entire night long, beaten violently. By sunrise I was at my end.

After a brief pause, all of the abuse began again, but this time I was not only beaten violently, I was dragged by my hair throughout the entire house and bitten all over my body. My grandmother, my partner, and my uncles who witnessed all of this were desperate and didn't know how to stop me as I was dragged from one side of the house to the other.

At a certain point, when things started to die down, my aunt Assunta hugged me and I told her all about my nightly vision - the person standing in front of the rectory of the church of St. Anastasia's. From the description I gave her, she immediately understood to whom I referred: "that's Joey, Angelina's husband."

At this point I don't remember anything else that happened after that. I only remember but I found myself in my aunt's bed, crying and not wanting to leave because I was tired of suffering so much violence and being beaten.

And then I heard Joey's voice, whom, most likely, my aunt Assunta had called. And then I found that I was on my side under the bed. He came in, grabbed my arm and pulled me out, subduing me on the ground.

I'm not sure what happened right after that. I saw Joey's sister Marina in the room and then Gabriel, his friend. I was manifesting strongly, trying to bite and scratch Joey in order to get me out of his grip. I was cursing him in one moment and then telling him not let me go in the next. He wasn't in the least bit intimidated and refused to give up, but began to pray and a strong voice with everyone present in room. They continued this until everything was calm again.

And then he took me in his arms and lifted me onto the bed, sitting next to me, praying, caressing my forehead. Finally, in that moment I regained my confidence and I understood that Jesus, through Joey, was showing me his love, using him as an instrument. I began to call him my guardian angel.

After I had calmed down a bit, Joey called the secretary of Friar Benigno telling him what had happened. He made an appointment for me for the next day.

From that moment on the disturbances increased and became more violent. The sexual violence and the bites became extremely painful. I had a painful swelling in my abdomen and genitals and it felt like I was burning on the inside, so much so that I was doubled over in pain. It hurt so much I couldn't even scream. The next morning, along with my guardian angel, my partner, and my grandmother Giuseppina, I went to Palermo to visit Friar Benigno.

And we came close to the church of St. Paul where he worked, and before getting out of the car I began to have a very strong aversion to the place, so much so but I didn't want to get out of the car, asking to return home.

But fortunately, Joey took me quickly and by force led me through the door to Friar Benigno, who was waiting for me in the vestibule. In spite of the strong sense of authority that he exudes, he began to calm me down with kindness. But I continued with my aggression and rebelliousness. Some medical doctors who work with Friar Benigno attested to the strange hardness of my abdomen.

FB:

It was December 19, 2014. In the first interview I was made aware of everything that Marianna has recounted up until now. I then proceeded with the exorcism prayer. The invocative exorcism prayer was accompanied by all of the typical reactions one finds in possessed people, and then she fell into a deep sleep. But as soon as I began the imperative exorcism in Latin, she woke up and stared at me. In Latin I asked: *"In Nomine Iesu, quid est nomen tuum?* (In the Name of Jesus, what is your name?")*. The response was, "Lucifer."

At the end of the exorcism her heart and abdomen became normal which brought Marianna a great joy. She could only remember some parts of the exorcism.

Marianna: After the prayer I returned home exhausted but smiling. It was late morning and as soon as I got out of the car, I went to the bathroom because I felt as if I had an object in my womb. I remember that I expelled something as if it were a stillbirth. It looked like a huge clump of blood, some parts dark and others lighter, it was in the shape of a fetus. I began to retch but I couldn't vomit.

In the days between my sessions of exorcism with Friar Benigno I continued to suffer the nightly sexual abuse, while the day brought beatings. During that time Joey was very close to me, physically, but especially with his prayer. Following Friar Benigno's counsel, my boyfriend and I decided to live chastely in preparation for our sacramental marriage. And with that I was able to receive Communion every day in Mass, nourished by the Word and the Body of Jesus Christ.

I rediscovered the joy of reconciliation with God through confession and, regardless of the difficulties, and with the help of Jesus, I was able to accept with serenity the trials I was undergoing.

Not denying that on many occasions I was tempted to spit the Host out of my mouth, I was, nonetheless, more strongly aware of the need I had to bear Jesus within me in order to have the strength to keep going. My motto became (and continues to be today): *I can do all things in Him who strengthens me.*

Often it would happen that during the participation at Holy Mass I had the sensation that somebody was touching me. This was very disconcerting for me and more than once it compelled me leave the church.

The month of January 2015 was particularly difficult and seemed interminable. I wasn't able to enter my own house and was forced to sleep on a cot in Giuseppina's house. It was enough to cross the threshold of my own house and I was thrown to the ground and dragged from end to end by my hair, systematically beaten throughout. The bites on my legs left scars that I still have today. My body was left covered with bruises. There came a moment when I told my guardian angel that I couldn't take anymore of the situation and that I was thinking of putting an end to it all. It seemed clear to me that my life in this world had only caused problems for me and everybody around me - nobody would miss me if I were gone.

Given my condition and because I was physically declining so rapidly, I was sent to undergo all sorts of medical exams, none of which revealed any pathology. As a result, they couldn't prescribe me any medicines. Curiously, the exams said I was in perfect health and none of the doctors could understand my obvious physical decline.

Even my boyfriend became quite discouraged and despairing, frequently calling Joey to the house in search of comfort and strength.

One day, when my body was being attacked, my body arched, moving and moving throughout the house quickly like a spider, frenetically – in all different directions. Suddenly, I fell to my knees and with arms extended turned towards the little room next to my bedroom and began to invoke in a strange language the names Venerius, Gloria, Asmodeus, Lucifer, and Satan[7], their leader. And then, turning towards my partner, I said, "It's useless to pray for her, she's mine and I won't let her go."

---

[7] Some theologians are of the opinion thati in Satan's fall, his punishment was to be be split in three personalities: Lucifer, Satan, Beelzebub – a fitting sentence for his non-conformity with the will of the Blessed Trinity.

One Sunday morning, Friar Benigno came to my house with Joey and my husband. After having greeted them initially, I distanced myself from him because he scared me, so I hid in my bedroom.

FB: I went to Marianna's place to exorcise her house as soon as I realized that it was undergoing a diabolical infestation. When I finished the exorcism, according to the ritual, I sprinkled the different rooms of the house with holy water. As soon as I reached a storage room, Marianna began to manifest and became very agitated. In it were several toys. When I picked up one of them her reactions increased. I took that toy to another room. I returned and I sprinkled the storage room with holy water again. This time Mariana had no reaction. We then went to the room where I placed the toy. As soon as I stood in front of it her cries of pain began anew. So, I took the toy and went out with her husband. I exorcised it, destroyed it, and threw it in the trash. Coming back in we found Marianna calm and particularly joyful.

Marianna: It's clear that Friar Benigno, enlightened by the Holy Spirit, was able to find the cause of my disturbances in that toy with which my son played everyday. From the moment in which he exorcised the toy and destroyed it, I started to get better and was finally able to smile. One thing stands out. On that beautiful, sunny day, Joey smiled at me and said, "Your face has changed, it's resplendent and you look peaceful."

I continued seeing Friar Benigno for several months more until the day of my definitive deliverance. From that time onwards, all of my disturbances ceased:

- I was no longer beaten, bitten, dragged around the house by my hair;
- The drawers and cupboards stopped opening closing on their own as they had so violently done;
- I was no longer stripped naked, bound, and sexually abused;
- The bruises scratches and bite marks ceased to appear on my body;
- The swelling and hardening of my abdomen and the burning sensation in my genitals came to a halt;

Everything disappeared except the memory of it.

Today I think God because thanks to this extremely painful experience I've begun a path of conversion. I form part of an evangelization team in my parish, and my team is led by my guardian angel, Joey.

To this I will add a sad note. Yet again my filial instinct led me back to my father. I had a strong desire welling up within me for him to participate in my wedding with Cyrus. In spite of all of the evil he had done to me, I went to his house in Trapani. My invitation was met with a curt denial. After a string of insults he added, "Get lost, you slut, I'll never go to your wedding."

Naturally, this caused me much suffering, and left me in a fit of tears. In spite of the circumstances, the Lord allowed me to remain serene, granting me peace of heart, free of any rancor whatsoever towards him. It was to be my uncle, my mother's brother, who would walk me down the aisle to the altar of the Lord, where my marriage with Cyrus was blessed.

Lord Jesus, today I want to praise, glorify and thank you for your presence in my life. And to you, Blessed Virgin Mary, with the same love with which you loved your Son, you love me too. Thank you, Mama, because through your intercession I have the strength to pardon everyone who had done me so much harm. And I thank you too, Friar Benigno.

Teresa: A deliverance, fruit of a promise to the Blessed Virgin Mary

My name is Teresa.

Everything began for me in July 2010. My husband and I were brought to desperation, at our wits end. After many fruitless visits to specialists owing to my intestinal and gynecological problems, life became impossible for me. I had become a prisoner in my own house, because the mere thought of leaving made me sick to my stomach, complete with spasms and continual evacuations.

I won't get into the details of my ceaseless cycle… Suffice it to say it consisted of continual hemorrhages lasting a week, then a pause for a week, and then it began again.

The doctors always sent me away telling me my tests looked fine and they were at a loss for what sort of an illness might bring about such symptoms as these.

In July 2010 I was invited to dinner with my husband's cousin because she wanted to tell me something. We chatted pleasantly throughout the evening until, at one moment, she mentioned that something wasn't right with me. She asked if I would go meet the founder of a prayer group, a layman whom she accompanied along with some priests, who did prayers of healing and deliverance. "Who, me?" "Yes, precisely you," was her response.

With a bit of diffidence I went to go meet this gentleman who did a prayer for me and suggested I come back with certain regularity because he knew there was something wrong with me. He suggested I go to the group he had founded so they could pray for me.

I went to this group twice on my own since my husband was not so convinced. Then he brought me to our parish priest, who, in his turn, convinced me that I should go to the Renewed Friars Minor at Saint Isidore di Baida in Palermo, where a certain Friar Benedetto work as an exorcist. He also warned me that it might be difficult for me to get an appointment with him.

So I tried. My whole family and I went and we knocked on the door. Who should open up the door but Friar Benedetto himself, who, with great kindness received us and listened attentively to my whole story. He asked if I was open to receiving an exorcism and I readily accepted, because I was in such need of help. To be honest, I had no idea of what would happen thereafter.

At first there were no manifestations. Nonetheless, Friar Benedetto asked me to go to my house and see if there was some object tied to the occult.

My mother told me that my maternal grandmother spent many years in a convent, but as soon as she left she found my grandfather and eloped with him. Then, enticed by some acquaintances, she began to visit psychics and fortunetellers for everything. Around the age of 16 or 17 my mother and my aunts also began to visit such characters. I then discovered that the union of my mother and father was the fruit of an occult ritual that involved the use of her menstrual fluids.

As a young girl I began early on to have problems with my menstrual cycle. And since I couldn't find a boyfriend what do you suppose my mother did? She brought me to a witch doctor in Monreale.

Shortly thereafter I met Giovanni, my husband. I continued to visit that witch doctor without telling my husband until the day he became suspicious and asked me why I was going to Monreale every two weeks. I told him that I was going to a witch doctor to solve my problems, since I often vomited and strange things were always happening to me.

As soon as I told him this, he brought me to Father Stassi, exorcist for Eparchy of Italo-Albanian Church in Sicily, whom I continued to visit for a while. The visits, consisting of some brief prayers, took place every six months.

Giovanni and I were married on May 10, 2003, after years of continual battle, arguments, but so much love. It was a beautiful day. Upon returning from our honeymoon, I had been reduced to a skeleton from the continual vomiting and the chronic evacuations in the bathroom. I attributed it to something I must have eaten.

And so began my married life. Three nights in a row my body stiffened up on the bed and I could see how I left my body. "I'm going crazy," I told myself, quickly running to the doctor. He told me it must be due to stress and that it would quickly pass.

That's when my true Calvary began: continual illness, frequent visits to the hospital, surgical interventions in the emergency room. During my first pregnancy the doctors discovered a polyp in my nasal septum. At times my blood loss was almost fatal. There were other medical issues, as well. But the most disconcerting thing was that the doctors couldn't explain what I had since my exams didn't match any of these symptoms. When I was sent to specialists, they were equally dumbfounded.

I began to have severe stomach problems, causing me to go to the bathroom between six and 10 times a day, and always with solid evacuations. My cycle never stopped. I went to different gynecologists and their response to me was always the same: "I can't find anything out of order." I became increasingly argumentative with my husband's family, even over little nothings. Further, I began having horrible nightmares in which I saw so much blood, and then the next day – or two days later at the most – I would learn that something horrible happened to someone in my family. About these things I spoke only with my husband. It filled me with anguish to know that something horrible was going to happen to someone before it happened.

In the meantime, we moved. The new house became my prison. I hated my husband, I hated the house. I was always stuck inside. It often happened that during the night I would suffer sexual violence from an invisible being. I thought I was going crazy but I couldn't speak about it with anyone until that day, that I already alluded to, when I spoke with my cousin.

And now we come to the last five years.

During the first encounters in which I received exorcisms from Friar Benedetto, there were no manifestations whatsoever that would make one think that there were grave diabolical problems at hand. But as the encounters intensified and as my prayer in the house with all of my family present increased, the evil author of so many continual disturbances was gradually unmasked. Over the course of three years I met with Friar Benedetto every week. During the first year he spent lots of time before each prayer session investigating and reconstructing all of the prior events that unleashed all of these disturbances in me.

My husband had to accompany me – with force - because as we approached the place where the prayers were done, I would always begin the manifest in attempt to escape. After a year of exorcisms I began to experience periods of physical relief, and nonetheless it became increasingly more difficult for me to come to Friar Benedetto. A thousand obstacles would always present themselves thanks to the insistence of my husband, I was able to overcome them.

During the last months in which I was helped by Friar Benedetto, my husband was forced to bring along my father because – as I mentioned – he was no longer strong enough to restrain me during my violent reactions and the exorcisms.

At a certain point it seemed that Friar Benedetto and my husband found one of the keys to my problem, and thus increased their prayer. Indeed, every time they prayed for the soul of my paternal grandmother, my reactions became increasingly more violent, screaming and wailings on account of the flames that were burning me.

During the nocturnal attacks I invoked the Blessed Mother, suddenly crying out her name, only to see a dazzling bright light arrive, freeing me from the grips of the Evil One. Since then I began had great difficulty falling asleep, Friar Benedetto suggested I use the time to pray. Thus, I would pray the Chaplet of Divine Mercy every night at 3:00 AM, and then plead incessantly to the Blessed Virgin Mary.

My reactions during the prayers were becoming increasingly stronger and more violent – at least that's what they tell me. I remember nothing of it.

It was suggested to me that I abandon my house for a little while to see if it was the house that was provoking all of my disturbances, but nothing changed. No matter where I went, I experienced all sorts of disturbances. I could hear noises and voices in my house, and see shadowy figures among other things. One afternoon, as I was preparing to go to a wedding, I ran into my husband, Giovanni, already dressed in his suit and we conversed a bit. A few seconds later, Giovanni came upstairs from the street. I looked at him strangely because he was still wearing his shorts. So who was it that I had just spoken with?

Another evening I was in the bathroom. My husband and my daughters were in bed and I began to hear the words: "Where are you going? Where are you going?" A little perturbed, I left the bathroom and I asked my husband what he wanted. He just looked at me as if to say, "You're nuts." He hadn't said a word.

Another thing that was quite strange: for weeks on end I could see a woman through my window watching me. The vision was so clear I could even describe how she was dressed. One morning, my sister-in-law, who lives next door, told me how she was worried because her three-year-old daughter would see this woman in the garden every evening, and she was scared. She didn't know whether to believe her or not. So she had my niece tell me everything about the woman that she was seeing and it matched up exactly with the woman that I was seeing every evening; I only suggested that they pray, "It can only help," I said. Little by little, the vision of the woman in the garden disappeared.

I became pregnant with Leo. I went to Lourdes and experienced no manifestations. In fact, I felt great during those days and my baby did fine. Upon returning to the doctor, he told me that the child I was carrying in my womb would certainly be born deformed. I was willing to accept anything, but Friar Benedetto reassured me that these were simply attacks of the Evil One. Indeed, Leo was born healthy, but shortly after his birth there began a long period of inexplicable illnesses - all mysterious to the doctors. One morning I was at home alone with him and suddenly I found him on the floor face down, crying. He had just turned two months old and was too small to move himself.

During one exorcism – so my husband tells me – I said that I no longer wanted to come to see Friar Benedetto. I invoked the name of my paternal grandmother who had died years before. I never had a good relationship with her. My husband also told me that when they prayed for her soul, the personality that manifested in me became very agitated and violent.

The years passed and the prayers of exorcism gradually brought about improvement. I read as I was able to (I was incapable of reading certain books because I would begin to lose control of myself), and I received Communion every Sunday. I managed to remain in church, but the problem was getting there. As soon as I walked in, seeing the statue of the Blessed Virgin Mary, I would say: "Here I am, I made it. Now help me to be strong." That's how it was every Sunday.

One day, Friar Beningo came to Palermo. He's also an exorcist, taking over for Friar Benedetto. I was very frightened of him and hated him, even before I knew him. I was told that it would be very difficult to get an appointment with him but lo and behold, Giovanni managed to speak directly with him and thus my exorcistic therapy continued. I immediately noticed that something was different in these prayers, they seemed stronger. Deep within myself I could appreciate and perceive this battle between the Devil and Friar Benigno. Immediately I would enter into a total trance.

My prayer life at home increased and unlike before, when it was very difficult for me to say the Rosary, I was able to pray it with greater ease, but not always. Although there continued to be constant disturbances, it was not like before, and sleep came easier. My husband intensified his prayer life, going to Mass every morning, and I knew that he did it for me. If I had not had his support during those years, I have no idea how it would've ended for me. But God has never abandoned me. Today, more than ever, I understand how much love my husband had for me throughout all of this.

In February 2015 my maternal grandmother died. The night before I had a dream of St. Rita of Cascia, who wept tears of blood. When I awoke I understood that something strange had occurred. I immediately grabbed my prayer book. As soon as I began to prayer to St. Rita, my aunt called me telling me that my grandmother was at the hospital in grave condition. She died after hours of silent suffering. With her passing, something changed in me. Things began to improve for me, especially in my spiritual life.

On May 7, 2015, the Blessed Virgin Mary appeared to me in a dream, majestic and looking upon me from on high, and she whispered to me: "Tell me what it is you want. Ask me, don't worry." I raised my arms and asked for the greatest thing possible: "To be definitively delivered." She looked at me and said: "before your wedding anniversary, it will be as you ask." My anniversary is May 10.

And on that day I was definitively delivered. With my deliverance everything stopped:

- The visions and voices ceased.
- The nightly visits from the evil one came to an end.
- My constant vomiting and visits to the bathroom stopped.
- I no longer had horrible nightmares.
- I stopped losing such large quantities of blood – and my gynecological problems disappeared slowly. Now I have a regular cycle, I feel almost normal. I received no medical attention for this. For sure, in the past doctors had given me different prescriptions, some stronger some not so strong, but not seeing any benefits they told me to cease all medication. One time I went to visit the gynecologist with my mother. At one point, she got frustrated and asked the doctor if, perhaps, it were better for me to go visit the psychologist. He responded in the clearest of terms that this was not a problem of that sort. Other specialists confirmed the same.

- My inexplicable hatred for my husband and my house came to an end.
- No more insomnia.
- I no longer experience difficulties going into churches or participating in Mass.
- Along with my manifestations, my hatred and fear of Friar Benigno also came to an end.

So many tears and so many prayers!

At the end of March, 2015, the month of the Blessed Virgin Mary, I could say, that when I looked back I could see so much darkness, for sure, but I also saw so much light.

Most certainly, I went through extremely difficult years – it's not easy being possessed! It impeded me from having a normal social life with other people; even the act of attempting to read a book was torture. I was only able to do whatever I did with the help of the Virgin Mary and a strong will. An example: Friar Benedetto suggested I pray the Rosary every day. But as soon as I began to pray, I began to manifest and vomit. Solution – I put a basin near my bed and I began to pray; when it was time to vomit, I vomited, but I kept praying. I did my part, but only with the Blessed Virgin Mary by my side to support me.

I'm convinced that, left on our own, we get nowhere. In isolation our hearts are arid, and cannot be transformed from hearts of stone to hearts of flesh. God has never appeared to me directly, but he has afforded me the opportunity to know wonderful people who were a great help to me during those years. All I did was open the door each time. From my own experience I can say that it's fundamental to be supported by those around you; those who embrace the Cross and carry it with you. In my husband I have found such a person; not to mention the Blessed Virgin Mary, Padre Pio, and St. Rita.

I cannot but praise the Lord for how He has worked in my life. I didn't know Him, but He knew me very well. By way of this tragic experience of diabolical possession, our Lord's plan was to bring us very close to Him. Today I can say I am truly in love with God. I cannot get along without Him, the necessary oxygen for my soul. I will always recognize the great good He has done for me, and the only way to live out this gratitude towards Him is to enter into this great mystery, which is God, and forever tell Him: "I love you, Lord. May your will always be done."

This diabolical possession turned out to be a grace for my husband, as well. What follows are his words:

Giuseppe: my wife and I only went to Mass on certain occasions: weddings, baptisms, First Communions, etc. But since we never lived in a state of grace we could never receive the most Holy Body of Jesus Christ. At Friar Benedetto's behest, the first thing we decided to do was to commit to Sunday Mass, to go to confession frequently, and to pray daily. Initially this was not easy, but today, after five years, my wife and I praise and thank God, because this diabolical possession helped bring about His plan for us. In the month of May, when we finally understood that what was happening was not a punishment, but rather a gift in the guise of suffering and trials. It brought us to truly know Him and, therefore, to be converted.

I cannot but praise and bless the Lord for everything He has done for my wife and me.

Lorenzo: Through exorcism, Lorenzo returned to being Lorenzo (and only Lorenzo)

FB: Lorenzo came to me the first time on December 30, 2014. During the initial interview it came to light that he had been hearing voices that suggested he commit very grave and negative things. But after he carried them out, he remembered nothing of it. When his wife would tell him what he had done, with stupor, he responded: "Did I really do that?"

He had an insane desire to have sex, but not with his wife. And with this intention he walked the street casting his gaze on a woman who would inevitably turn around. Furthermore, when leaving for work he would always get lost. One day he heard a voice that said to him: "Do you want money? In exchange, I want you."

Often he would become paralyzed while lying in bed. He was frequently beaten by an invisible entity, leaving his body covered with bruises.

He also told me that he had certain powers that allowed him to foretell the future occurrences – things that would always end up happening.

One day he treated his wife horribly, but remembered nothing of the event. During the prayers of exorcism his manifestations were extremely violent, his eyes beaming hatred for me. One day, he managed to wring the neck of one of my late team members. Of course he remembered nothing of it. On August 6, 2015, he came to receive the prayers of exorcism once more. For the first time there were no manifestations and he was able to participate in the prayer. What follows is his testimony.

Lorenzo: recalling the events of these past years and setting about writing a testimony with regard to them almost paralyzes me with fear.

In the month of August I experienced a great misfortune and a special grace that don't often occur in the life of practicing Catholic: the misfortune of seeing the Evil One, and the blessing of seeing the light of God's goodness.

On August 6, for the umpteenth time, I joined Friar Beningo for the prayer of exorcism. Unlike the previous occasions, I was able to make the responses to the prayers, to pray with calm and fluency, without trembling, without agitations, without feeling the Devil within me. Those who accompanied me during the prayers of exorcism and who had witnessed my extremely violent reactions were relieved: I returned to being Lorenzo, just Lorenzo.

It is not easy for me to recount everything that has happened to me, because some of these things I've heard from others. For days on end I would be out of myself, my body did not obey Lorenzo, but it did obey someone else.

The memory that torments me is bound up with the day I first knew Evil. It was in 1995. My mind is still filled with the atrocious image of seeing my father in bed, possessed by the devil, being thrown about. Coming close to him, I felt a hot wind come over me accompanied by an infernal sound and laughter. That's when I came face to face with evil and I began to live in perpetual fear. Even after the death of my father I would continue to hear that same laughter.

In 1996, well traveling through Sicily for work reasons, I had a head-on collision while going around a curve. My mouth was filled with blood. A gravelly voice whispered to me: "Stay here and you'll be mine." I felt lots of heat throughout my body and could smell sulfur. Then I fainted. I came out unscathed.

After that I grew professionally. Working in sales and marketing for the municipal administration, I was a machine: I traveled endless miles, going from town to town, with almost no recollection of what I had just done. Together with two other colleagues - my partners today - we decided to go into business for ourselves.

I went out with several women and that's how I got to know my wife. Oddly, she was the only one I found it difficult to be with. Today I know why: she has deep faith. We got married in 2003 and I can say that during the preceding months I had to fight against a strong temptation to call off the marriage. So much bickering! It got to the point that we almost broke up a few days before the wedding. But thanks to her and her forgiveness for my faults, we were able to celebrate our wedding. I can still remember that in the moment of saying, "I do", I lost my voice and my throat burned, even though the rest of me felt fine.

Most mornings I would wake up fatigued, because during the night I fought against people and animals that were trying to attack me. A few days before my wife lost our child through miscarriage, I dreamt of blood and saw a baby being taken from me while I was tied to a chair and unable to move or do anything. That was 2004.

I had another car accident with my business partner alongside me. We were saved because minutes before the accident I saw it all happening in my head, and knew what I would have to do to save us. That same laughter I heard before came out of my mouth throughout the entire accident.

Accompanied by much fear from the previous pregnancy, in April of 2005, my daughter was born. It was pre-announced by a voice that told me it would be a girl.

Meanwhile, I was getting more and more nervous, isolating myself; something was tormenting me, inviting me to leave everything and runaway. The real torture began about four years ago. I saw dead people who invited me to go with them. I stopped going to church and receiving Communion. I began using curse words again and refused to visit cemeteries because of the voices that tormented me there.

Having to fight against those voices that wanted me to abandon my family and change my life forced me to expend enormous amounts of psychological energy. This all played out in my body, which began to deteriorate. I experienced sharp pains in my stomach. The clinicians said that I had the stomach of an old man. Then, in 2011 I was diagnosed celiac. In my rationalism I no longer believed in God or His Church.

Then, out of the blue, my health improved. My reaction was to become became arrogant, presumptuous, and even a bit evil at times. My greed for greatness brought me to the point of obsession regarding the acquisition of a factory in Venice. I went against everyone in order to realize my dream. But in the end, for very strange but flimsy motives, it did not come to be. I was destroyed and embittered, feeling condemned to remain in Palermo. My rage transformed into a hatred for everything.

One Sunday my daughter began her classes for First Communion, but to me, the Church and Mass were a dead letter. I used the excuse of being celiac for not receiving Communion.

Meanwhile, I began to lose weight again, but I felt fine. My body was always in movement and it seemed that I was on a course of self-destruction. In order to have an alternative source of income, I purchased a bar. I remember that night of the acquisition: I was beaten by an invisible being, punished because I ought not to have bought something that would bind me to Palermo forever.

If before I passed unnoticed by women, at that time it seemed that many pursued me. Sometimes, I was able to read their minds, seeing their desire to have me. I could tell what people were thinking in order to anticipate them. I used these "gifts" to benefit my work without the least scruple. For days on end I acted in an unconscious state, without remembering what I did or said. And when others would tell me what had happened, it was the first I knew of it.

Until that point I was able to resist the desires of these other women. But one day I met a woman and I lost my head: divorced, lots of family problems, and a daughter who was the same age as my daughter. Something was pushing me to betray my wife and I couldn't stop it. My longing to use her was insane. Sometimes I cried, because I was afraid for her. I was no longer in control of my body of my thoughts. For months she was in love with me. I was no longer having relations with my wife. I had an urge to leave my house, never to see my daughter again.

One day a message on the cell phone made my wife aware of the whole truth. In a heartbeat, she threw me out of the house and I left.... Laughing that old laugh. But the strange thing was that on that same day, and with great malice, I also abandoned my lover. That was October 2014. After having used her, abused, and leaving her possessed, I destroyed her. One evening I explained everything to my wife, telling her that I needed to see my daughter again.

I told her everything that was happening to me, even about the suffering I had brought upon that other woman – who, by the way, felt so offended, she wanted to destroy me. That was when I began to ask pardon from God. That was also the night that I was beaten mercilessly by an invisible entity. Everything was going so poorly for me but I wanted to die.

I began receiving exorcisms from Friar Benigno. In the first prayer the evil spirit within me came to the surface.

In December I came back home. My wife, still offended and sad about everything that I had done, received me because she understood what I was going through. But one evening in March I treated her so horribly - I remember nothing of it –she had to lock me in the bathroom. The next day she threw me out of the house. She was afraid that I would do something harmful to her or our daughter. I went back to my mother's house, where I lived in isolation.

With each prayer of exorcism I entered into a trance and knew nothing more. I was subsequently informed that during the exorcism I reacted violently to the prayers of Friar Benigno, trying to punch everybody that was holding me down. Coming back home after the prayer I was thrown onto the ground and beaten by an invisible being. My vomiting was continuous as was the smell of sulfur.

I began to go to Mass again, receiving the Eucharist, but it always put me in a bad way. I prayed as best I could.

Along with Friar Benigno, a Carmelite friar named Giusto from the Church of our Lady of Good Help, accompanied me spiritually. He taught me how to pray, exhorted me to confess frequently and forgive everyone. Subsequently, I found my lover and I asked her pardon, but I could tell that something entered into her during our relations. She was still madly in love with me and attracted to me and all of my wildness, but I distanced myself from her, I wanted to have back everything that I lost: my family, my life, my mind.

Back at my mother's home that night it was a real battle: those invisible beings were destroying me physically. In my sleep they suffocated me and I always woke up covered with bruises. I was so afraid. Even my mother was afraid because she perceived what my problem was but didn't know what to do for her son.

Even if I was destroyed physically, I continued working and I wanted to keep fighting. I remember a brilliant light during the last prayer, like a laser penetrating me, and from it came a sweet voice.

During the prayer of July 23, I remember that, unlike the other times, I didn't feel the urge to react to the prayers of exorcisms as I did before, I was lucid, could listen prayed along with the others. On August 6, 2015 I went to receive the prayers of exorcisms without any attempt of escaping. Everything took place with tranquility; I was free. From that moment on all of my disturbances came to an end:

- The anger and hatred for my family and for anybody close to me ceased.
- No more insomnia.
- The nightly and daily beatings from the Evil One are a thing of the past.
- I no longer wake up with bruises and marks on my body.
- I no longer vomit upon reception of the Eucharist.
- I no longer desire other women.
- There are no more fugue or disassociative states.
- I can no longer read the minds of the people I meet.
- My dreams of dead people I've come to an end. No longer do I smell sulfur.
- And lastly, my desire for self-destruction has disappeared.

I continue to see Friar Benigno once a month for an exorcism of support. Now, I go to Mass every day, I pray (how I love to pray!), and I no longer feel so negative all the time. I'm a new man and I'm working to win back my family.

One last thing: as of a month ago, I can eat normally, with no celiac limitations or disturbances or desire to regurgitate food as before. I'm still awaiting the results of my latest my blood test. And all of this occurred when, one evening, I heard a sweet voice whispering my ear that I could go back to eating normally.

I thank everyone who has supported me to not carry out the will of the Evil One, which would have resulted in my destruction. I also pray for everybody I have ever harmed.

God is great and He truly exists.

Thank you, Lord!

Sofia, delivered through the intercession of Father Matteo La Grua[8]

My many sufferings seem to be related to the period in which I was in my mother's womb. It turns out that my father's grandmother, a renowned occultist, imposed her hands over my mother's belly.

Already in my infancy I began to suffer disturbances. Now I am 48 years old. I can remember, that as a child, I would sometimes see the floor suddenly covered with beetles, frightening me and causing me to cry a lot.

At the age of four years old, while in the house of my maternal grandmother, I played with two other children who were older than me. The devil appeared to us three, like an old man with horns, suspended in mid air. From that day onwards my life became hell: full of physical and psychological torments. I began to have a fear of everyone and everything, incapable of sleeping in my room alone, or of being alone to study, or even of walking home alone from school. The situation deteriorated so much when my mother, in an attempt to help me, brought me to occult practitioners. Everything became worse once my father joined a prayer group of renewal in the Spirit.

---

[8] Translator's note: Father La Grua ofm. Conv. enjoys the fame of sanctity throughout Sicily and much of Italy. He was a tireless exorcist who exhibited heroic charity. He was also gifted by our Lord with some extraordinary gifts. An example: one of Friar Benigo's team member recounted to me that she had been living far from the sacraments. Upon learning of the death of her father, she ran to the first church she could find in search of consolation. She saw an elderly priest she had never seen before. Before she could say anything, he called her by her name and told her not to worry about her father. But recommend she pray for his soul since he was in purgatory and needed her prayers. That priest, Fr. Matteo La Grua, would become her spiritual after that.

In spite of the aforementioned, my mother and I also became participants in this church group, which began to pray for me. At this point, the presence of a curse in me had not yet been discovered. Nonetheless, the more I grew spiritually, the worse the manifestations became, having to spend days on end in bed, not wanting to leave my house for fear of everyone. Of course I visited doctors and psychiatrists, and they prescribed strong doses of different sorts of medicine that only made me drowsy. There were no positive results.

When I was 18 years old, while participating in an encounter of different prayer groups, I met a young man who would become my husband.

Even after our marriage, the manifestations continued to afflict me. I would wake up fatigued in the morning, bound and pummeled by obsessive thoughts. In spite of the suffering, the Lord granted me the gift of two beautiful children who had to be practically raised by my mother, since I was not in the psychological or physical condition to do so.

When I had just turned 23, and after a very intense but brief bout with illness, a deep nostalgia for my father grew within me. And this longing, saddled with my afflictions, cast me into a very dark place. But when I turned 40, everything came to a head – and speaking of heads, I thought mine would explode. Thinking they were helping me, everybody would ask me, "So why are you in such a bad way? You've got everything." After all, I had two wonderful children, and a husband and mother who adored me.

Not seeing any other way out, along with my family, we made the decision for me to go to a psychological ward in Florence where I would be hospitalized. In fact, there were two periods in which I was hospitalized, subjected to very strong medicines, lasting a period of two months. The doctors agreed that my illness was atypical. In fact, during the periods of hospitalization, it was as if I had left my problems at home.

In January 2009, I had the good fortune of speaking with Father Gabriele Amorth, who told me that the devil often manifests through such obsessions. As a result, he told me to seek out an exorcist, suggesting I see Father Mario in Caltanisetta. In the first session of prayer with Father Mario, he determined that my physical and psychological problems had no origin in natural pathologies, rather it was a demonic problem.

One day when I was in Caltanisetta, awaiting my turn of prayer with Father Mario, two young men inquired where I came from. And when I told them, they told me there was no need for me to make such a long journey to receive exorcisms because Friar Benedetto worked as an exorcist in Palermo. In that moment, something very strange happened: a second after the two young men spoke with me, they disappeared from my view.

And so my weekly sessions of exorcisms with Friar Benedetto began. After Friar Benedetto was transferred to Corleone, there came a time when I was receiving no help whatsoever. One night, Father Matteo La Grua came to me in a dream, asking me how I was doing. I remember that dream vividly and how I told him everything I had endured. He listened attentively and then said, "It looks like we will have to start from the beginning." Two days later, without having called anyone or mentioned it to anyone, I received a telephone call from Friar Benigno's secretary who told me that Friar Benigno was already familiar with my case because he had accompanied Friar Benedetto in some of his exorcisms. She gave me an appointment.

FB: It was November 27, 2013. In the first interview, beyond those things I already mentioned above, Sofia told me how it was quite difficult for her to go to Mass, and that her participation in Mass brought about so much suffering. She experienced hatred for people she did not even know, suffered from a sort of narcolepsy, continuously heard blasphemies uttered in her ear, couldn't bear to be touched by her husband and, as a result, matrimonial relations became a very difficult – and when they did have them, she would see in his face the faces of other people. She also felt a continuous nausea,

She also told me that in her home things would break on their own, she could foresee things that were about to occur, that she felt sick during Mass and that violent blasphemies increased during Mass. She told me that after receiving exorcisms from Father Mario and Friar Benedetto, certain disturbances had disappeared. As a diagnostic I began to do an invocative exorcism. Immediately, she entered into a trance and manifested all of the typical signs of a diabolical possession, the demon told me his name was Asmodeus. My secretary, who had been present for Sofia's exorcisms with Friar Benedetto's exorcisms and was present in this one, claimed that the violent manifestations were stronger this time.

When she came to the next appointment, she remarked how, upon returning to her house after the last exorcism, the pains in her body were worse then before. Soon after that, participating in the Mass of the Solemnity of the Immaculate Conception, she could feel something crawling up her back. After that, she experienced back problems and, at times, was strangled by an invisible presence that brought with it a burning sensation deep within her bones.

On May 6, 2014, when commanded during the exorcism, Asmodeus told me that there were seven spirits present in total.

Sofia: Amid the ups and the downs, always trusting in the Lord, I returned periodically to receive the prayers of exorcisms from Friar Benigno. We come to 2014, and to be more precise, the month of October.

One day, as I sat in the waiting room for my doctor appointment on Gaetano La Loggia Road in Palermo, I struck up a conversation with the woman next to me. She was accompanying her mentally disturbed brother to the doctor. During the conversation she mentioned that that she went to the Capuchin parish near the cemetery, where Father Matteo La Grua is buried. I knew him well from the time when I was a youth going to the prayer groups and she suggested I go visit him.

After the doctor appointment, I felt mysteriously impelled to visit the Capuchin cemetery. But when I arrived, to my great disappointment, the custodian told me that the cemetery was closed for maintenance since it had to be prepared for the approaching feast of All Souls, and as a result, it was impossible to enter.

I broke down in tears and, perhaps moved by my tears, the custodian suggested I write a note for Father Matteo. With tears in my eyes, I wrote out my note explaining to Father Matteo what my needs were, asking him to intercede with God for my deliverance.

From that day onwards, everything changed – for the better, of course. The disturbances diminished until such point that they completely disappeared. Finally, I could go to Mass without suffering and participate in all of the parish functions with great fervor. The tremendous sufferings that I endured: the horrible blasphemies in my ears, the repulsion and the nausea, the disgusting smells that tainted the air, the narcolepsy, and the utter hatred for everybody around me all came to an end.

The proof of my definitive deliverance took place during Eucharistic adoration in the Church of St. Vincent in my hometown. I had a terrible cough caused by bronchitis when I went to the church, but during the adoration, for an entire hour, I was enraptured by Christ, never coughing once. As soon as I left the church the coughing began again. I even had a cough during the next prayer of deliverance that Friar Benigno continued to do over me until such point that he could affirm: "It looks like there's nothing there anymore, you've been delivered."

During those subsequent exorcisms, there were no more physical disturbances and I was able to listen to everything Friar Benigno was saying, even praying along with him; while in previous exorcisms there were some brief moments of lucidity, but I remember almost nothing of them, coming out of the trance only with great difficulty and fatigue. My husband, who was present during the exorcisms, would tell me what had occurred, the horrible words and blasphemies that I uttered, the insults directed at Friar Benedetto and Friar Benigno, and the constant retching and vomiting.

Through the grace of God and with the intercession of Father Matteo La Grua, I am a new person. My life is changed and none of those disturbances have returned. Every day I experience the need to pray every day. I love to go to daily Mass, living each day with joy, even though one needs a bit of grit to confront life's problems.

Before ending, I turn my mind and my heart to the Lord with great gratitude for the gift of granting me deliverance. Thanks are also owed to the priest exorcists who, with great sacrifice and abnegation, spend themselves physically and psychologically, using the strength God gives them so that people like me, afflicted by such evil, achieve rebirth to a new life.

Carol: deliverance after five years of suffering

FB: the first time Carol came to see me was on November 29, 2013. During the intake interview it came to light that she had been helped by an exorcist over the last year, Friar Benedetto. She explained how she would wake up every morning at 3 AM and find it impossible to fall back asleep again. She saw dark figures and also what seem to be people all around her. She could hear heavy breathing and other strange noises in her house, only to find broken objects in the morning. She was often paralyzed in bed, unable to move. She felt like she was being observed in every moment. She had been suffering these disturbances for the last three years, but the week before our meeting, at 3:30 AM, an invisible presence began to abuse her sexually, unto penetration.

Her mother, a practitioner of occult rituals, told her that these were good spirits. The mother, in spite of her sudden and drastic changes in personality, had quite a following of people who claimed to benefit from her services. A heavy drinker, she could finish a bottle of whiskey in one night without showing any signs of intoxication. She had hoped to pass on her powers to her daughter who was unwilling to receive them. She was also quite a possessive and authoritarian figure, claiming that she would be the one to decide who Carol would marry. But since Carol had eventually made her own decision, she refused to participate in the wedding, she showed up in front of the church with sacks of rocks to throw at her daughter.

Carl's disturbances began immediately after her wedding. She had problems in her sexual relations with her husband – rejecting him for no reason whatsoever. And when she did have relations, it was only at the cost of tremendous pain, beatings on her stomach, on her neck, and swelling in on her let cheek and part of her throat. The beatings were accompanied by strangulation.

As soon as she would enter into a church she was filled with fear. And upon receiving Holy Communion she reported sharp pains in her mouth and stomach, the need to vomit, her head whipping around and a strong sensation to spit out the Eucharist.

Her reactions during the exorcism where quite strong, entering into a trance immediately. When commanded, the possessing demon claims to be Lucifer, indicating that another spirit was present, but he refused to say the other name. My team, made-up of a forensic psycho-pathologist, two general practitioners, and an educator with the background in psychology and pedagogy for borderline cases, accompanied me during the long interview with Carol and then were present for the exorcism. Everyone was in agreement that this was a case of diabolical possession, and not an example of psychological pathology.

Before we hear from Carol, we shall let her husband speak:

When my wife began to have problems, Father Mario Cascone counseled us to seek the help of an exorcist. We went to Friar Benedetto and, with him, began the prayers of exorcism, taking place every two weeks and lasting 15 minutes each session. As soon as Friar Benedetto began to pray in Latin, my wife would go into a trance. I would always stand behind her, but when Friar Benedetto placed the crucifix on her head, war was unleashed – nothing less than a true fight. She began to shout and exhibited a force as if many men had come together for the same purpose. I was aware of her suffering and I suffered along with her in silence, fighting for her with my prayer. The sessions never lasted longer than 15 minutes on account of the many people who are awaiting their turn. At the end of the prayer I carried her in my arms backed the car. She had such problems walking and even moving, but little by little she would come back to herself overtime and need to rest afterwards.

Every night – so my wife would tell me – she had to fight against the Evil One. But I was never around because this happened at 3 AM every morning and I was already at work, such that my wife was left on her own. Upon my return from work, I always found her in such a horrible state after her long fight. Often her attacks began even before she went to bed. As soon as we would begin to pray, she would either become drowsy or enter into a trance, become irritable and so agitated that I would have to physically restrain her. I would then pray over her and thanks to the good Lord's help she would calm down.

Carol: at the age of 12 years old, I remember that there was a constant coming in going of people at our house, who, together with my mother, locked themselves in a room, but I did not know what they were doing because I was not permitted to enter.

In the course of a day the stream of people coming to my mother for her so-called "novenas of prayer"(I don't know what they were exactly) was rater constant. They seemed to be some rituals carried out for days on end.

Every morning she incensed the whole house using a cooking pan filled with charcoal, a little incense, a clove of garlic, and some alcohol. This was not the classic type of incense used in church ceremonies; it produced a large flame. If the flame died down, she added more alcohol. She went from room to room reciting a sort of prayer and then, in every corner of the house, she sprinkled holy water that her cousin brought her from Lourdes.

In the dining room she had a little statue of the Blessed Virgin Mary surrounded by other little statuettes. She would often like candles to them and a taper had to be lit for a certain period of time, below which she would place of photograph of the person indicated.

She had a large crucifix that she used to bless the house, her business, and for her "prayers". She also used to use a large wooden crown, placing it on the person over whom she did her rituals.

We children, of course, didn't go to Mass because our mother didn't train us in the faith. The exception was my brother Vincent who went to Mass with frequency, and even wanted to become a priest, but my mother would not permit it.

Amongst this continuous retinue of strange people that visited our house, were people like Flavia the tarot card reader – whom we also went to see at least two times a week; "Uncle Johnny" the healer who lifted curses and always paid my mother for more "novenas" in exchange for the help she gave him; and then there was the woman name Vita who was my mother's right hand in charge of drumming up business for her.

When I turned 14 I noticed that my mother began to show a very dark side of herself that I had never seen before. I would see her face change and she would begin to speak with a male voice. The voice told me that I shouldn't be afraid and that he, the spirit within her, was a friend of my mothers.

I grew fearful, always looking for excuses not to be alone with her because I did not want to know her world as it disturbed mine so much.

Some years after that, Concetta, my brother Vincent's girlfriend, was at home and asked my mother for help. So they brought her to Father Stassi. Only after several attempts were they able to get her to enter into the church where he was offering Mass and once inside, she began to swear at the priest with masculine voice.

Once the Mass was over, Concetta was supposed to visit with the priest, accompanied by my mother and my brother Vincent. Less than a minute passed when she ran out of the church, screaming that she never wanted to see him again. And so my mother asked her to sleep at our house in order to have more control over her. Frightened, every little noise made me jump that night since I had never seen so many strange things in one day.

From that day onwards I began to pay more attention to things and ask myself many questions: "My mother drank so much but never got drunk. Why was that?"; "How did she always have so much money if she never worked?"; "My father was a simple laborer, where did all this money come from?"

In order to help me overcome my fear, my mother began to reassure me, saying that she helped people by agency of good spirits. That did nothing to allay my fears. She confided in me the names of her four spirits, informing me that, should the need arise, I, too, could call one of them who would always come to my assistance.

That's what I began to have strange visions: at home and outside.

The part of the house that most frightened me was the living room such as it was: entering, sitting on a couch on the right side was a doll whose eyes moved and there were two figures of knights facing the window; on the left there was a small boudoir with three porcelain dolls who looked real and that my mother strictly forbade anyone to touch; and finally, before the balcony there were another two knights. They, too, faced outside.

My mother described these four knights as "the guardians of the living room." Whenever I was in that room, I always felt like I was being observed and sensed that I wasn't alone, tremendous fear welling up inside me.

Often, when in the countryside, I would lose my senses and get lost, but with one of the prayers that my mother taught me, I was back to myself. Whenever one of my siblings would become ill, she began making a sign of the cross over the affected part, then applying her mouth to their head. She would begin to touch the affected parts of the body and then the head. Whenever she did these rituals, she made sure that the room was closed tightly, and then, opening the windows, breathed out the air that she had aspirated from the sick sibling, always ending by closing the window.

That was a period when, during the afternoons, she would sit me down and with crucifix in hand, apply it to my head, saying: "Tell me your name, I command you." Of course I would look at her as if to say: "you're nuts."

After several tries, she would tell me that since I didn't have any being within, she would offer me one of her own. I responded: "I don't know what you're talking about and you're making me afraid with all of this. I don't want to hear anymore about this."

She became enraged and I, in order to distance myself from her, got a job because I couldn't stand being around her anymore. That's why I would only see her in the evening when I got home.

At the age of 15 years old, my brother's friend asked me if I wanted to spend my life with him. My mother was delighted, but not I. His name was Luigi and he was 25 years old – the age difference was too much for me. At that time I liked to hang out with my friends, to play, so how did I end up becoming engaged him? He smothered me with gifts to the point of drowning in them. If I went out he would tell my mother because she had to control me in all of my movements. I couldn't stand it anymore so I cut myself off from him.

And that's when my Calvary began. That's when my mother began to show her hatred for me: she stopped preparing my meals, washing my laundry, folding my clothes, because I, just this once, didn't follow her plans. This situation lasted a year.

And so I spent a large part of my adolescence hearing my mother tell me how useless I was; a mistake whom she had attempted to abort several times. Since she had been unsuccessful in this, her wish was that I would die during childbirth - even if it meant her death, too.

Every time I had a boyfriend she would find out and scare him off. My friends were very frightened of her. Since she was so controlling and possessive, as I grew I took the decision to avoid her completely. Thus, I no longer saw what she did for work but I was certain that she was continuing to do what she had always done, because the telephone calls after dinner for the "novenas" were incessant.

When I turned 19, I met the man who would become my husband, often meeting with him in secret. One day he had a motorcycle accident requiring surgery and I figured we wouldn't see each other for days. So that's when I decided to inform my parents officially about my engagement. My mother treated me to a royal engagement. She really liked Antonio at first, but after two years began to have an aversion for him. She didn't want me to see my future mother-in-law because she wasn't part of the family. Then she began to build up this negative image of Antonio, claiming he was drug addict and a thief – definitely not good enough for me.

Of course, I did not believe her. I knew him quite well because we worked together and I was certain that none of what she told me was true. Nonetheless, in her malice, she forbade us from seeing each other.

But Antonio and I loved each other and we couldn't stop seeing each other. As a result, we had to do it secretly. When my brothers learned that nothing had really changed between us, they decided to drive me to and from work in order to keep me from Antonio. In spite of them, we managed to see each other.

We argued very much during the space of nine months that we had to come to a decision whether we would stay together or separate for good. Love triumphed and we eloped.

I called home to let them know that I wasn't coming back and my mother responded: "Do you understand what kind of a mess you got yourself into? Now it's clear that you deserve all of this. I wish you every ill in the world and I hope that God does not give you any children or, in the case that He does, that they'll all be handicapped."

After two months I found out that I was pregnant. I let my mother know to see if this would calm her, but it only engendered more curses.

She called me up five months later asking if I had seen the ultrasound. When I said that we had, she responded: "Good, now tell me how bad his deformities are."

After that I didn't want to hear from my mother ever again. The fact is, I was the one who was getting quite sick during the pregnancy.

After seven months together with Antonio, we decided to get married, in order to live in God's grace. I called my father because I wanted him to walk me down the aisle, but he said he would have to ask my mother first. My mother kept him on a short leash, only doing what she allowed him to do. As expected, the response was negative. My mother did not give him the permission to walk me down the aisle.

Since everything was turning out so badly, we informed the priest who was accompanying us in our marriage preparation. He said not to worry about it, go ahead with your marriage. I found out that my mother had already planned to bring sacks of rocks into the church in order to throw them at us. As a preventative measure, security was placed outside of the church to impede her entry.

After nine months, our daughter was born and my mother even came to the hospital to make a scene there. We had already forewarned security to ensure she couldn't bother us. She claimed that her daughter was taken from her and nobody was letting her see her daughter. She even said, "Just let me see her suffer during childbirth and then I'll leave." Four years later, and thanks to the help of some of our relatives, we reached a degree of peace.

My mother had to undergo surgery for the removal of a tumor. During the surgery her medical aide told us that it was useless for us to wait in her room because our mother would have to go to intensive care. And yet that was not the case. The doctor said: "This is a miracle, God has saved you," but she reprended him with vigor, patting her her breast, "No, with my own strength, and no one else's help."

The day before she left the hospital, I went to clean her house and in her bathroom cabinet found two notebooks: one of them was hard to reach and the other was in a shoebox along with pictures of many people, ourselves included. There were several shot glasses and some writings called "special novenas." Each novena was accompanied by a picture.

The picture that shocked me the most was the one of my engagement with my husband: we had left it at the sanctuary of St. Rosalia along with a note of our petitions. And in that moment my whole world fell apart. I couldn't understand how she came to have that picture and what she would do with it. I panicked, grabbed everything, and took off.

I began to be afraid of everything.

From that moment onwards, my mother began to look for reasons to argue with my husband. Every day, at a different time, she would show up to take me out. I no longer had time to care for my house. Rarely was I at home when my husband came back from work, and that's when my terrible headaches began.

Since my husband and I rarely saw each other during the week, my mother would often send over food she had cooked. More and more my headaches became unbearable, but then I also began to have sharp pains in the neck of my stomach. I visited doctors but with little success; they couldn't explain where the disturbances were coming from.

After several weeks I met Josephine, a good friend and a sister in Christ. She invited me to a prayer group that was meeting that very evening. "Some other time," was my response. In spite of that and feeling awful, my husband and I ended up going.

It was there that I discovered I had spiritual problems of a diabolical nature. This caused me to come closer to God and to distance myself from my mother – not because I no longer wanted to see her, but because my commitments with the Church kept me away from her and I was no longer available for her daily visits. This infuriated her.

Now we come to the year 2010, when I began to have prayers of exorcism with Friar Benedetto.

Every night at 3 AM I had nightmares and I was attacked by a "presence". I was a mess.

Often I had problems going to the houses of friends and relatives because of my manifestations. The presence of certain people disturbed me greatly. But I decided not to give up the fight, asking God to be close to me and give me the strength to confront whatever came my way.

I wasn't alone in this. I had my husband and an entire community along with me on this journey. They prayed for me and supported me.

I noticed that distancing myself from my mother actually made me better and I couldn't understand why. One day, while speaking with Father Mario Cascone, while on a spiritual retreat, I told him my whole life, getting off my chest everything that had caused me so much suffering. And that's how we discovered the true source of all of these disturbances.

Coming back from the retreat, I spoke with Friar Benedetto and we made an appointment for him to bless my house and see if there was something that wasn't right. We ended up having to empty our whole house because everything my mother had given me carried her "baggage."

After some prayer, Friar Benedetto understood where my problem was coming from. He prescribed me a few drops of exorcised oil on a tiny piece of bread every day for my stomach problems.

This was a difficult road because I began to experience hatred for my mother. Everything became onerous for me, but amid the suffering and the inconveniences everybody close to me was of great help.

It was very difficult for me to pray but I was able to do so with the help of my husband; I went to Eucharistic adoration, daily Mass, and prayed the rosary everyday to support me along the way.

The prayers of exorcism left me destroyed, a real mess for several days afterwards, with pain throughout my whole body. I felt as if I had been run over by a truck.

I went to confession every week in order to ensure that my heart was free, but the telephone calls from my mother were constant and unbearable. They frightened me as she heaped curses upon me.

The last thing I heard from her was: "You're all going to die of a tumor. You and your families are cursed." She also told me that my husband was going to end up in a wheelchair, unable to feed us, living under a bridge as a beggar. So I decided to change my telephone number to avoid further such phone calls.

In the last years I ended up going to Friar Benigno to receive my prayers of exorcism. That's when I began to see the first improvements.

But one night, a night filled with disturbances there was something that bothered me more than everything else. Satan was able to make me believe that he had had sex with me. I felt him touch me, caress me, up to the point of feeling dirty and no longer worthy of my husband. The next day, Friar Benigno explained to me how the evil one works on our minds to make us see and think things that are not so.

After several years I received a message for my sister-in-law through which we were able to be reconciled. My brother, by the way, was also receiving prayers of exorcism from Friar Benigno for the same problem. Together we approached our brother Carmelo letting him know that our distancing ourselves from our mother was not without reason: we told him everything. Thus, he too, joined us on the path of faith. After 20 years he went to confession, and now goes to Mass every Sunday and Eucharistic adoration every Friday.

After five years of suffering, thanks be to God, I experienced my deliverance.

At last:

- I am able participate in Mass without any problems and actually quite moved by it;
- I no longer reject my husband;
- I no longer have problems in matrimonial relations;
- I no longer have a squeezing sensation in my neck and stomach;
- I sleep fine now; but if there is the slightest attack, I can defend myself with prayer, without the sense of panic I had before;
- I no longer have strange visions;
- I can now visit with people without experiencing disturbances;
- I can pray without falling asleep;
- I no longer have constant headaches that send me to bed.

I continue to be a member of the Burning Bush Community of Prayer where perpetual adoration of the Eucharist has become a source of ineffable joy. The graces I have received in prayer have completely changed my life, helping me to leave behind me everything I have suffered. I've been made anew, a new person.

Ever since my dialogue with Friar Benigno, I constantly pray for my mother's conversion. Even though she claims that what she only does is good for others, everybody on the receiving end suffers. The only thing to do for her is to pray.

Friar Benigno continues to see me once a month - but not just me but fifteen of us who have received the grace of deliverance, return to him to receive prayers of deliverance.

Alleluia. Alleluia. Praised be Jesus Christ.

Beatrice: Our Lord brings about wonders from a spiritual problem

Throughout my life, and that of my husband, God was always in the last place.

Our marriage was not a happy one, and at times we discussed the possibility of the separation. As our children grew up, our relationship with them became quite difficult as well. And to complicate things even more, my husband experienced continual work problems, bringing with them the contngent financial hardship.

More than once the idea crossed our minds that misfortune followed us and there was no exit. In spite of the many invitations that my mother-in-law made to us to come closer to Jesus and trust in Him, our response was, "No thanks, will make it on our own...."

In September 2009, our life fell apart with the news that our son's girlfriend was expecting a baby. We were confused and disoriented, but nonetheless, we welcomed them into our home, counting on moral and material support from our own parents.

The situation was not easy and after some months it became even more complicated when my son, owing to some health problems that the doctors couldn't figure out, was compelled to take a leave from work, eventually losing his job.

Amidst the thousand difficulties, the months passed and Christian was born. In February 2012 the child, who could speak quite well for his age, began to manifest strange behaviors: he screamed and cried, seeing danger everywhere. One day, while we were visiting our cousins at their home, a Franciscan friar who was a friend of theirs came to bless the house. We took advantage of his visit and asked him to pray for the child, explaining all of the problems that he was undergoing. He did so, following it with a blessing over everybody. What next occurred was the last thing that I could have expected. I began to feel pain throughout my entire body, so much so that the priest had to interrupt his blessing. He invited us to visit his friary and during the prayer that he did over me, again my body suffered all sorts of horrible pain, making it difficult for me to breathe, then I lost control of myself. All of this is what was told to me because I have no recollection of it. The same phenomena repeated themselves with each prayer.

Finally, that Franciscan friar, who was not an exorcist, suggested we contact Friar Benigno, because he was sure that I had need of an exorcism. It was not easy to contact him. Months passed and in the meantime we began a journey of faith, going regularly to Mass, albeit I had to leave the church at the moment of the consecration, because I would lose my breath and the pain was too much.

I also went to receive prayers of healing and deliverance, but especially I went to Eucharistic adoration; and all of that with extreme difficulty and only with the patience, the perseverance, and the sacrifices of my family: my husband, my sister-in-law, my mother-in-law, and my mother.

Some of my brothers and sisters in Christ, especially some from the charismatic renewal, to which my sister-in-law and mother-in-law belonged, invited us to participate in their prayer group, even knowing what my situation was: with great faith and courage they stayed close to us with their constant prayer and physical presence, letting us know that we were heard and loved: the things I needed most.

In the month of October we met the Friar Benigno. After explaining my situation to him a bit, he did a prayer. Immediately, I was gripped by horrible pain to the point of crying out, gasping for breath, I then felt like I was being strangled and couldn't speak anymore.

In light of these symptoms, Friar Benigno organized a meeting with his medical team. After a conversation and examination, the team accompanied Friar Benigno in the exorcism, during which there was tremendous pain throughout my entire body and there came a moment when I lost control of myself completely. My husband, who was present, tells me that I began to turn my head in a strange way, my legs gamboled about, as I screamed my responses to whatever questions Friar Benigno put to me with a harsh, almost masculine voice.

That was the beginning of my exorcistic therapy with Friar Benigno and renewed journey of faith for me and my husband. Besides Mass, we began a life of almost constant prayer, with the adoration of the Eucharist every Friday at the charismatic center "Gesu Liberatore" in Margifaraci founded by Father Matteo La Grua, where there were other people who suffered the same malady as I did.

There we met Father Daniel. He too was very important for me because he often spoke about the need and the importance of forgiveness. We prayed the Rosary together and, at the end, went before the tabernacle to thank Jesus.

Although it was not easy, we continued along our journey of faith. The Evil One tempted me (and those who accompanied me) with discouragement in many ways, but the prayer support of so many brothers was the source of our strength. It encouraged us to continue forward and persevere in the fight for freedom.

Two and a half years had past. One Friday in the month of February, we went to Margifaraci for Eucharistic adoration. As was the custom, they had a Eucharistic procession. I felt a very strong need to ask Jesus to heal my heart, to the point that I could forgive everyone that had ever done me any ill.

When the Blessed Sacrament approached to me, this longing became even stronger. When He was in front of me, a powerful heat passed through my entire body, leaving me with a profound sense of peace.

Thinking that it might be a deception of the Evil One, we decided to make nothing of it. Similar things had happened in the past causing me to think that I had been delivered, only to be let down upon finding that the devil was still there and stronger than ever. Consequently, before coming to a positive conclusion about what had occurred, we went to our next session with Friar Beningo.

As I recounted everything, Friar Benigno listened attentively and then proceeded with the prayer of exorcism. The pains in my body were greatly diminished, my breathing was a bit easier, and most importantly, I was able to accompany him in the prayer for the entire time. Finishing up, and with a smile, Friar Benigno told us that my deliverance had begun.

My deliverance continued concomitantly with my path of faith to the point that now, after three years, I am completely delivered. All of those disturbances that I had suffered during the prayers and the Holy Sacrifice of the Mass have disappeared.

From my spiritual problem of a demonic nature, the Lord was able to bring about wonders, strengthening my faith and that of my husband, immersing us in His merciful love and finally granting what my sister-in-law what she, with so much love, had implored: our conversion. For all of this and for everything that our Lord has yet to give us, I praise Him, I bless Him, and I thank Him. Alleluia.

Gertrude: Delivered at the foot of the Cross

FB: Gertrude, a married woman, began coming to me for exorcism on March 20, 2014. In our first conversation she explained that she had been going to another exorcist for the last four years: Friar Benedetto. During the prayer she would always fall into a trance.

Her problems began in early 1991. She got mixed up with a man who claimed to have special powers and spirit guides, maintaining that they helped him do positive things. She was involved with him for 15 years, ensnared the whole time. One day he brought her to Gibilrossa, near Misilmeri, for a "prayer". Another time, he brought her to Isola delle Femmine, a small coastal town built on a cliff, where he did a strange ritual involving fireflies in which he summoned up a vision of a large ship, visible to all of the participants.

As time passed, the man died and whatever problems had in the past seemed to pale in light of her new situation.

The man began to come to her in visions at night, saying: "You have to come with me." Of course, it was not the man who was appearing to her, but the devil in the guise of that man. At first these apparitions were limited to conversation, but then it evolved into nightly sexual relations – always at the same time. With the prayers done by Friar Benedetto, this phenomenon disappeared completely.

Proceeding with the invocative exorcism as a diagnostic tool, Gertrude entered immediately into a trance and exhibited the typical reactions of a possessed person. In the following months she began to improve, but continued to have the visions like clockwork. She would see a ship approaching and a voice that called out to her: "Come with me." Every night at 3:15 she awakened, trembling.

Gertrude: 21 years ago I began my Calvary. I was in a very bad way. In my mind I was convinced that I was being helped by a man whom I knew carried out occult rituals. Although I thought he would be a blessing for me, it turned out to be quite the opposite. As the years passed the problems multiplied, ever more aggravated by the fact that I was increasingly becoming identified with my own sin over those 15 years.

After his death things became extremely complicated, as if the entire world had imploded for me. The only lifeline to salvation was a friend of mine who helped me to discover the Word of God.

Between 2007 and 2008 I began my association with the *Oikos* groups, but the situation became even more complicated. I was incapable of seeing any light of salvation: my life was always filled with tribulations in so many trials, above all in those last years.

In 2010, the priest sent me to Friar Benedetto, a very kind and welcoming Franciscan exorcist. During my time with him it seems that this was a road with no exit; it was as if evil were feeding upon itself. He blessed my house and I got rid of everything that could have been contaminated by that man, anything associated with him or possibly cursed by him.

People suggested that I go to Marian shrines to find my deliverance, but my financial situation did not permit this. I saw my refuge in prayer alone.

Nonetheless, in July 2012 I was able to go to Medugorje for the first time. I went on my own, without my family, surrounded by very special people who did everything they could to help me. I received so much from each one of them.

There was not a church or a holy place in which I did not confront the Evil One. The shrieks on top of that mountain were indescribable; every single station of the cross threw me to the ground – everything was a spiritual battle. When I finally came back to myself, at first I couldn't remember anything, but after a few hours, little by little, my recent reactions to everything began to take shape in my memory.

Coming back to my family, things only got worse. It was as if I were one with the evil within me: it never left me in peace, and I was constantly agitated. It was as if prayer brought about no good fruits for me.

A year later I returned to Medjugorje with two of my daughters. I was in a bad way the whole time, discouraged and calling out to the Blessed Mother: "Why all of this evil? How much more do I have to suffer?"

In March 2014 everything reached a crisis point. Thanks to the good counsel of the priest, I turned to Friar Benigno to receive exorcisms from him, because Friar Benedetto had been transferred to a friary in a different diocese. Every appointment with him was a continual battle – the evil one did everything to kill me and I was getting worn out; but thanks to the help of the good God, I was able to persevere, dealing head on with my situation.

The disturbances caused by this evil entity day and night brought me to the end of my rope. I no longer wanted to live. I had become its sexual plaything.

I began to pray asking that my family and I would be able to return to Medjugorje together in August of 2014. And so it was.

We climbed Mount Pdbrdo. Even there I began to manifest, but not so badly as in earlier trips, only falling two or three times. But as I approached the foot of the statue of the Blessed Virgin Mary, I entered into a trance and lost all consciousness.

Two days later we climbed Mount Krizevac, where I experienced the greatest pain I have ever felt. The crises of manifestation that brought me to the ground were less than before, but I was destroyed as I approached the cross. Embracing it, I let out a scream. I remember almost nothing of that moment, in fact, only one thing remains in my mind: I cried out to the Blessed Virgin Mary asking her to deliver me and come to my aid.

Coming back home, I continued my sessions with Friar Benigno, who noticed something different in me. I no longer had the reactions as before, nor did I enter into a trance anymore. I continued, however, to see him for the next few months for exorcism.

In April 2015 he suspended all further prayers because I had been freed.

With an exultant soul, Virgin Mary, I am here to give you my most heartfelt thanks. You knew how to open within me the infinite treasure of God's merciful goodness. In my need, you came to my help; in my pain you brought me comfort, in my desire, you obtained from your son the grace of deliverance. Now all of my disturbances have ceased, and I'm doing quite well. I ask you never to abandon me. Your help is always with me that may I use the divine gifts for my salvation and to the praise of the Blessed Trinity. Amen.

Greta: From Visceral Hatred towards Everybody to the Glory of Deliverance

My name is Greta. My story began some 12 or 13 years ago. I already knew Friar Benigno back when I was a daily Mass goer. But my home life, thanks to me and my husband Francesco, was full of chaos, insanity, absolute disorder, bickering, lies... Enough to make the Evil One gluttonous. We lived in a marriage far from God.

As soon as he tried to bring some order into the chaos that was our marriage, all hell broke loose.

Everything began during a moment of intimacy, something that was very rare if not to say nonexistent. My husband's face no longer looked like his own. He no longer looked like himself, rather like some horrible demoniac.

I mentioned this to Friar Benigno and he tried to calm me down, saying: "Don't worry, I'll just give you a blessing now and you'll see that everything will turn out fine."

I remember nothing of that blessing. What I do remember, though, was a visceral hatred for Friar Benigno and my husband. That day was the beginning of my Calvary, complete with prayers of exorcism every 7 to 14 days. This was a period filled with suffering such that the world cannot understand, let alone bear. The thing that most disturbed me was experiencing hatred for everybody: hatred for my family, hatred for the Church, hatred for everyone.

That's when my night disturbances began: every night, I was spontaneously awakened from the most profound sleep, almost always at 3 AM, finding it impossible to fall back asleep.

We were impeded from having a conjugal life and, when this did occur, my body would expel my husband. In those moments I entered into a trance and Francesco, my husband, would have to fight within an entity he did not know.

For a long time I slept on the couch, because the mere presence of my husband maybe manifest. It was a time of insanity, fear, terror: televisions and radios would turn on and off during the day and the night; we would find our mattress (which we have switched out three times!) rotated and leaning towards the ground, always on my husband's side.

One time we decided to go away for a week to try and relax. I was feeling better and I thought it was the occasion for a little intimacy with Francesco. I should've known better. As soon as I had these thoughts, I began to experience sudden and excruciating pains starting on my back and then throughout my entire body. I told my husband and even the blood in my veins was painful to me - it was a horrible experience. I tried to take some medicine but it had no good effect. The next day the pain continued and even got worse when I set foot in a church – it was Sunday. I took three pills right before Holy Mass, but it was useless. We had to return home.

A few days later I went to my doctor and described to him the pains that I experience. He asked if I'd suffered some sort of trauma, because it was impossible for pain to come out of nowhere. All of the exams he did for me came out negative; there was nothing that should have brought about such suffering. He concluded with, "This is inexplicable."

Meanwhile the prayers continued. I was not always conscious, but rather entered into a trance. At first, I felt paralyzed and then I lost all awareness. My husband would have to tell me what happened during those sessions.

After every prayer, whether it was a long session or a brief one, I felt fatigued, as if I had been run over by a tank.

In a certain period I was feeling very discouraged. Towards the end of each exorcism, as I was regaining consciousness, it felt as if a breeze passed through my veins, bringing me peace.

During one of the many prayers, Friar Benigno told me: "Greta, fight. You have to be strong." That was when the Evil One was trying to discourage me even more. Cut I treasured his words. I understood that the Evil One, by discouraging me, weakened me psychologically. Further, this gave him permission to leverage it against me during the prayer, subordinating me and emerging, coming to the surface.

Thus, my fight against him began. In every session I strengthened myself, seeking to fight with all of my willpower, trying to listen to the prayers and repeat the ones that Friar Benigno recited, not allowing the evil one to emerge. The pain caused by the devil did not cease, but now that I was conscious, I was the one that was doing the fighting.

Today, after so much unhappiness, so much suffering, and so much sorrow, I do not know how to thank the Lord, my sweet Jesus, for having shown me his mercy.

Thanks to the prayer, said to the Lord by a priest during his first Mass after his priestly ordination, imploring my definitive liberation, today, 13 years later, it is finally a reality. Thank you, my dear Jesus.

It's been eight months since I received the infinite joy this gift brings. My night insomnia has ceased. The mattresses stopped moving. Televisions and radios no longer turn on and off on their own. Francesco and I love each other. I no longer experienced hatred for him or anyone. All of the disturbances, the pains, and everything else, has come to an end without the help of medicine, but only the intervention of our Lord Jesus Christ.

FB: Greta's husband Francesco was present at every exorcism, sharing in his wife's suffering along side her. He is a true example of uncommon fidelity. Let's listen to his testimony.

Francesco: Everything began in 2003, when Greta began to experience strange illnesses of an inexplicable nature. After a series of clinical consultations that shed no light on the subject, we decided to speak with Friar Benigno, whom we already knew. We met with him, explaining to him the episodes Greta was having, having an effect on our marriage. He tried to calm us down, saying that with a blessing everything will be fine, but precisely on that day in 2003 our real suffering began.

I remember when that moment of simple blessing was transformed suddenly into a prayer of exorcism. In fact, I saw Greta change completely: she growled, rolled around on the ground, spat out insults at Friar Benigno and me. In that very moment my whole world came tumbling down, because I didn't know what was happening or what to do. I remember at one moment during the prayer, I had a violent reaction against that entity, still unknown to me, shouting at him and aggressively asking what he wanted from us, and from Greta in particular. I also commanded them to leave her immediately. I should never have done that, since, as it was explained to me, that is something reserved to the exorcist.

After the prayer, Friar Benigno instructed me on how I was to behave during the prayers of exorcism. He then explained to me that Greta was in need of exorcism.

I must say that my faith and my religious practice were almost nonexistent, but in that moment I began to pray and to believe deeply in the omnipotence of God. Further, having had the misfortune of being in his presence, I came to believe that the devil exists.

An example:

I remember one time, coming home from work and coming into the house, I saw Greta seated on the couch, her face darkened, with an odd look on her face. Immediately I understood that this was not my wife, but nonetheless I approached and I gave her a kiss. I remember how that one kiss set off an argument that was supposed to make me lose my patience. I did everything possible to avoid it, but during the discussion Greta (or whoever it was that was within her) touched on my weak point, my mother. In that moment I lost all control and mental clarity, and started screaming. I felt within me a fury that was growing and I understood that, should I continue, I would have done some irreparable damage. Then, in a moment of lucidity, I had the strength to leave the house, slamming the door. Immediately after that I heard it reopened and I saw Greta on the porch, with her face transformed, emitting an evil and mocking laugh, saying: "I've finally done it."

In that moment I understood my defeat: I allowed that unknown but malicious entity who had taken possession of my wife to lure me into a fight. I understood then that my only weapons could be prayer, faith, and patience. But these aren't easy things to do. After this experience I was able to confront such things that happened in my house with the greater serenity. And as I did so, my faith grew.

I have another recollection: during one of the prayers of exorcism, one that lasted around an hour and a half, I experienced deep emotions upon seeing the unnatural way my wife was suffering at the hands of the devil, causing such horrible pains in her whole body. I was also greatly impressed upon hearing the invective against Friar Benigno, and seeing how she banged her head against the wall. I tried to restrain her to avoid her harming herself anymore. At the end of this very long prayer, at the point of temporary deliverance, I saw Greta's peaceful face, full of light and serenity. Tears of joy welled up within me and in the other team members.

The most difficult episodes for me to bear as Greta's husband were those very rare moments of matrimonial intimacy, in which the devil physically impeded our union. Quite often it happened that during our conjugal act, the devil manifested in the very moment of my ejaculation. I could feel the body of Gréta expelling me, and I could see how her body became rigid as she went into a trance. The demon manifested speaking threats against me. I remember the first time this happened: I simply did not know what to do. I saw Greta after the phase of the trance, wiping away tears because she was tormented by the excruciating pains in her uterus. This terrifying moment traumatized my state of soul to such a point that I was afraid to unite myself with her. Not without suffering and embarrassment, we discussed this with Friar Benigno. And he, with great calm and tenderness, suggested I continue trying to have relations with her, and should the demon manifest, I ought to pray to the Blessed Virgin Mary to intercede with her Son for Greta's deliverance.

Today I'm convinced that God permitted events that brought about such tremendous physical suffering for Greta and so much suffering for marriage in order to bring about my conversion.

Today, after 13 years, in light of Greta's definitive deliverance, I rejoice in the new life that God the Father has granted us.

FB: To conclude it is fitting to hear the testimony of the priest who prayed in his first Mass after his priestly ordination for Greta's definitive deliverance.

Father Marco Di Maria: On the morning of April 7th or 8th, during the week of spiritual exercises in preparation for my priestly ordination, walking up to the Hermitage of Montecasale, I sat on the side of the street to enjoy the view and to pray. I felt joy and peace. In a certain moment, I felt the presence of the living Jesus with me; I sensed He was smiling at me. It was as if he were revealing his satisfaction upon seeing me there shortly before becoming his priest. But it seemed that He was asking something of me, something He longed for, something that would give him great joy. And this something would not be just for me, but for Him above all.

On the morning of April 10, during my first Mass offered after my priestly ordination, as I was seated (I don't remember if it was after the homily or after Communion) I once again felt the living presence of Jesus. Content and smiling he said to me: "And now I want to give you a gift. What would you like me to do for you?" I didn't know what to request. To be honest, in that moment I was praying for so many people and so many different situations. But then, suddenly, something came to mind to ask Him: the definitive deliverance of a friend of mine named Greta, who for years has suffered a diabolical possession. "Lord," I said, "let Greta be definitively delivered." I immediately sensed that the Lord was smiling as if to say that that would be the gift He wanted to grant to me. From that moment onwards, I had the certainty that the grace had been granted, but I mentioned this to no one; rather simply awaited confirmation. Two months later Greta called me, telling me how after Mass of April 10 at which she was present, all of her disturbances suddenly came to a halt and she felt totally and definitively delivered.

To Jesus Christ our Savior, whose mercies never cease, be all honor, glory, and unending thanksgiving. Amen.

Josie: her return to the Catholic Church

FB: Josie landed at our "Listening Center", motivated by some of her family problems. As a young girl, she became a member of the pseudo-religious "organization", but after many years and many battles, the Lord granted her a return to the Catholic Church. Here is her testimony.

Josie: The "organization" to which I belonged, not unlike many others, promised to make something great out of you, guaranteeing that you would become an autonomous, independent person, with absolute control over your own mind and body; it promised perfect consciousness.

My time in that sect was long and fatiguing, and I was able to get to a point in which I possessed certain powers, which supposedly lie dormant in our human nature, but in truth, such powers are channeled to diabolical means. Without the aid of hypnosis or drugs one begins to see mental images that supposedly come from a past life or are taking place at that moment elsewhere. One also begins to experience the phenomenon of telepathy, the ability to read the faults of others, the development of the so-called sixth sense, among other things. All of these powers have an inebriating effect, bringing with them a gratifying sense of omnipotence.

Using the methods that I learned, I was able to make a paralyzed man who had been in that state for more than 30 years, walk again; in the first moments after which somebody was clinically dead, I resuscitated him; I healed some people in a coma and I brought an infuriated crowd to a halt.[9]

Today I know that such powers were demonic, offering me mind control of myself and of others. I was assigned a demonic partner who whispered inside my head, making me think that the visions, the perceptions, and the consciousness that he gave me were my own. And the more I believed it, more power I had – power to control my life, becoming their perfect soldier

---

[9] I'm reminded of Luke Chapter, in which the enraged crowd attempted to throw Him off the precipice. Christ took control of the demon moving the people. He simply walked through them. Simillary, a possessing demon can communicate with the demons influencing others and make them do his bidding.

Up until a few months ago, I was convinced that the key to my power lay in the techniques that I applied. Today I know that that is not the case. I've been able to verify this: since further attempts at giving such commands no longer work. I remember the techniques and I attempted to apply them. If those powers had been given to me amongst the other resources of our human nature, the same results would still be possible. Yet this is not the case.

These efforts at attempting to acquire powers that grant euphoria and a sense of omnipotence are quite dangerous as my own experience has proven. Furthermore, they are open windows granting the Devil permission to enter into our own sphere of life along with his extraordinary action. And that's exactly what happened to me.

FB: Everything Josie relates raises the question of how she was able to leave the sect and come back to the Catholic Church. Here is her answer:

Josie: What happened on the night of Holy Thursday, 2014 radically changed my life and that of my family.

Actually, everything began in September 2013: I heard a voice within my head that told me to end it all, to kill myself while I was driving, but I was aware that such a thought could not come from me, because regardless of the problems I had in my life, I always loved my life and considered it a gift.

The insistent voices worried me. I thought that I must have some sort of a mental illness and so I spoke about it with an evangelical friend of mine who suggested I read Psalm 91 everyday, even if I didn't believe in the Holy Spirit and in God the Father, or even the devil. She told me: "God loves you and from this, in Jesus' Name, the Holy Spirit is with you. Every time you invoke the power of the Blood of Jesus, he will come to help you."[10]

Although I undervalued that, along with some of my friends, I decided that I wanted to get to know God, even if it meant going through hell to do so. And so we began to get together to pray our prayers, spontaneously, asking the intervention of the angels. In that moment a series of strange events began to occur: kitchen appliances started going crazy, I began finding a holy images upside down, demonic images superimposed on the pictures of my children, and above all, my daughter Helen began to get sick, weakened also by a strange allergy. The medical exams showed nothing anomalous or anything that could explain such reactions.

In April 2014, around a week before Easter, things worsened. Because of the enormous consumption of electricity in my house, we were in capable of keeping up with the bills and they cut off our electricity. In spite of that, we decided to remain home.

Around that time, my husband had a dream one night that he fought with the devil and began to throttle me. Upon waking up he could remember nothing of it.

My daughter Helen would speak a strange language during the night and even answer my questions, but in the morning she had no recollection of it.

---

[10] The economy of salvation and justification, and certainly the sacramental system, do not operate in this fashion.

I began to despair. A voice in my head told me to kill my children, leaving me infuriated. This was the day before Good Friday.

My little girl Helen had a fever and so my mother suggested I take her to bed with me. With the candle lit, I began to pray mentally in order to not wake up the children, but she, with eyes closed, asked me to stop praying. I turned towards her and took her temperature that was now extremely low at 93.9. Doing everything I could to not make noise, I continued to pray in my own way to God the Creator of heaven and earth, He who can do everything. But Helen became enraged and commanded me to stop. Suddenly I understood that it was not Helen who was speaking to me. Instinctively I responded: "I will pray for her even harder," beginning to pray in a loud voice, expecting the others in my family to wake up.

This new entity cried out: "NOOOOOOO!!!" Telling me that I was his, that I belonged to him because of a pact I had with him, which, if I didn't respect it, he would take my daughter Helen.

Meanwhile the candle blew out, the cell phone died, the door slammed shut and I could go longer open it. I cried out but nobody could hear me. All I could hear was a dog barking. I was overcome with panic, and I fell my knees, making sure that I kept my back to the mirror. I took Helen in my arms and kept my son Ivan in view as he slept. The new personality simply laughed at me through the mouth of my daughter and I, to try and help her, attempted to use the techniques that I had learned in the cult. It didn't work.

That new personality speaking through Helen used a language I did not know but, strangely, I understood. He showed me a desert. I knew that I was in the bedroom, but I could feel sand under my feet. When I asked him who he was he told me, "Beelzebub."

I didn't know who Beelzebub was, but I did know that if I didn't give him what he wanted I would lose my daughter forever. I almost gave in, when I remembered the words of my Evangelical friend and shouted: "May the blood of Jesus descend upon me and my loved ones, covering Helen. And in the name of Jesus Christ my Lord, may the Holy Spirit descend upon me and come to my aid now!"

What I saw was extraordinary. The entire room was lit up with a comforting light and I saw a sword of light cut the darkness, and angels floating in the air with swords of fire. The cries of terror were halted by the voice of my son Ivan, almost laughing: "Stupid demons, don't you know that angels are stronger?" I understood that my children heard me and I told them to pray in their minds and to repeat together with me the Our Father, which I couldn't really remember after so many years away from the Church, so I tried with my own words.

After a moment (it seemed eternal) everything calmed down and my daughter Helen, yawning, said: "Mom, I'm back." The door opened, the cell phone turned back on, and the sun began to light up the room; it was 5:45 AM.

The first thing I did was pack up my children and leave the house. But only after telling my husband what happened. Weeping, I went to my mother and recounted everything to my eldest son who, unbeknownst to me, had abandoned the cult and entered the Catholic Church. He brought me into a church where there was a certain Father Macario, who received me with great kindness. I told him that I was in a bad way and he asked me what religion I was. I told about my experience. "Don't worry," he said, "we'll take care of everything. Meanwhile, start praying." And he taught me, among other things, how to pray the Rosary.

During the subsequent days my daughter Helen would go in and out of herself, and the seven of us would simply pray the Rosary. As a result, I felt stronger and less isolated.

After that evening I made the decision to never turn my back on Jesus again, even if I didn't understand the nature of the disturbances that happened to Helen and not to me. That new personality that emerged in Helen was telling me that I belonged to it, but how could I if I never believed in the devil and was not aware of having addressed him.

Meanwhile, I had a big problem to resolve. I was outside of my house and we couldn't get in: the external security door wouldn't open and the dog in the yard was going crazy, I looked for a priest willing to come to my house to bless it and, if, hopefully, resolve the problem of the door that couldn't open. But no matter where I went, they told me that no one was available in the moment at the parish: the priest from my neighborhood had fallen in front of my house and injured himself and was not able to leave the rectory; the priest in another parish was busy with some appointments and couldn't come; the priest at a third parish, perhaps out of fear, decided to send a religious in his place, who did prayers of deliverance.

The Curia gave me the number for the only exorcist – their words - who could help me in this case: Friar Benigno. I called the number but his secretary told me that given the amount of appointments he had, he could only give me an appointment for July 9, 2014, and we were then at the end of April.

Once again I remember the words of my friend who told me "if the Holy Spirit has helped me when I was unfaithful, he will help me now as well."

Thus, armed with a Rosary, my husband, my son Giovanni, my daughter Martha, and I were finally able to open the door with ease, simply by praying the Rosary. The first thing we did was calm down the dog. We decided to no longer live in that house and change our lives.

Certainly, today our lives are quite different. Today I understand that the devil considered me his, and indeed I was thanks to my experiences in that cult. Not being a member of that sect was not what caused these most recent problems, but rather when I began to pray; that's when he came to claim what was his - my soul in exchange for the life of my daughter.

But why her out of the five children that I have? I finally understood when I remembered that, during my pregnancy with Helen, another member of our sect told me that his friend was about to die. He asked if his friend could be reincarnated in my daughter, since we believed in the phenomenon of reincarnation. My thoughts were first of all that it would be good to help somebody; secondly, I was proud to be asked; and thirdly, I thought that my daughter would have the ability to remember a past life, with all of the knowledge and possibilities of that other spirit who would lived in the other person.

The truth of the matter is that's the devil came to dwell in my daughter in the moment of her birth. In fact, when she was born she was covered with sores. The same phenomenon occurred with Giovanni, my oldest son, who is now 18 years old. During that time I was a dedicated member of the cult and my son turned out to have great abilities and psychic powers which today, entering into the Catholic Church, he clearly had to renounce – but not without consequences. But that's a story for another time.

Today I thank God for everything that has happened, for the word of God is true: *We know that all things work for good for those who love God* (Rom 8:28). I have been reborn to a new life and today I know much more now than before, when I thought I knew everything. I experienced the strength of the Holy Spirit who is far greater than any power we can think we can obtain. Nonetheless, this battle is not over for me.

Thank you Jesus, because you have always been at my side.

Jerry: a sorcerer who definitively renounced the practice of magic

FB: To end this chapter, I present you one last testimony. This person who had professional occult practice, the source from which came the presumably good spirits, thought he was doing good for others through them. That's how he described it to me. One of the spirits claimed to be in charge. He had them within himself night and day, at home or walking down the street. Without even wanting to, he could determine what somebody's problem was upon meeting him, since the possessing spirit would inform him about that person's situation and the nature of the problems he had so that Jerry could help them.

But Jerry, who liked to be in charge, wasn't disposed to receive commands from the spirits. Much the contrary, so he thought, he was giving them to the demons.

As we have already said, there are no good spirits that possess a person. If there are other entities in a person, they are always evil spirits, that is, demons. As a result, when Jerry thought he was helping people, he was in fact, and without knowing it, working for the demons, at their service.

And those people who turned to him seeking help, indirectly prostrated themselves before the demons at work within him, rendering them false worship: that was the price they paid to receive such benefits.

In our first encounter, among other things, he told me that those eight spirits were always present in him. Sometimes he would give commands to other spirits to make themselves present in his body. In order to do this he used his wand that had been given to him by another sorcerer. The strange thing is that he also used a crucifix and commanded "in the name of God" with it. What a paradox! The name of the same God who commanded us precisely to *not practice divination, consult soothsayers, augers, and sorcerers* (Deut 18:10-12).

Clearly, in this context the command "in the Name of God" was not an expression of faith, but was used in disobedience to the word of God and as a profanation of His holy Name, reducing it to a magic formula at the command of a wand. The crucifix Jerry used was not a sign of faith, of love, or trust, but rather this to was reduced to the status of a magic wand.

After the invocation and using the wand, Jerry would receive instructions from the spirits about the nature of the problems that a particular person had and what he ought to do to resolve those problems. The instructions that he received always involved magical rituals that he had to execute, that had their own particular efficacy. Indeed, he healed some sick and freed others of evil spirits. Without knowing it, Jerry was a sorcerer in the service of demons.

The price he had to pay for obtaining such results was his estrangement from God through his disobedience of the word of God, through the profaning of the holy Name of God – reducing it to a magic formula, the profanation of the crucifix, and finally, the cult rendered to evil spirits who, pretending to submit themselves to him, were in truth binding him to them.

I explained all of this to Jerry and I could see how his eyes were opened to a reality that he never expected. Little by little, he began to understand the gravity of his situation. The only reason he came to me was because he claimed that he and his family were under attack from some evil spirits and the suffering seemed interminable.

What was most moving in all of this was how God, rich in mercy, restored him to grace. He renounced those spirits once and for all. He renounced having ever used magic, even if he thought he was doing something good for others (so-called "white magic"). Nonetheless, such renunciations – as he told me – were not easy to do, in fact it was very difficult for him.

He decided to go to confession and brought me all of the objects of his work including his wand. Today he goes to Mass every day and receives Communion. He has also joined a church group to deepen his faith and do charitable works for others.

What follows are his own words.

Jerry: I consider myself very fortunate for having met Friar Benigno, who helped me discover my true identity. I had been successful in life and felt strong around everyone else. In fact, to be honest, I was a bit arrogant because I believed I had the following powers:

- The power of secret knowledge;
- The power of spiritual sight;
- The power to do anything to resolve the problems of others, especially when they were sick. I was sure I was helping them.

The reason I went to meet Friar Benigno was because of what I was going through at that time. Many strange and painful things were happening, one right after the other – not so much striking me, but my family. When my wife spoke with an acquaintance, she was counseled to contact Friar Benigno who might be able to help us.

The first time I went to the "Listening Center" for our dialogue, they explained to us that all of the problems we were undergoing were most likely caused by me, on account of the situation I chose to live in, and they made an appointment for me with Friar Benigno.

In the first encounter with him, he asked me many questions and then did a prayer of blessing and that was that, offering me another appointment. While I was on the way back home with my wife, I told her:" I really don't want anything to do with that friar, he doesn't really understand what we're going through."

Nonetheless, given the insistence with which my wife exhorted me to return for a second appointment – and then in that moment discovering that Friar Benigno was an exorcist - I decided to go, if only to make her happy.

The second time he prayed over me the spirits within me were unleashed: I began to speak in a strange language and became very violent. I kept on turning towards the open window: looking up into the sky well I saw myself and someone else with Friar Benigno who were arguing. And from within myself there came a singular evil. My brain could only produce hatred and fury. I would have destroyed everything. I looked angrily at Friar Benigno and, if I could have done him harm, I certainly would have. I felt stronger than him. Nonetheless, there was something like a barrier that prevented me from touching him. I thought to myself: "Why is he not afraid?" I was conscious the whole time but more as an observer, sitting on the sidelines and unable to do anything.

Along with Friar Benigno was a woman who prayed for me. I turn towards her and said all sorts of things in order to frighten her, but she continued praying and didn't pay any attention to me.

After a good long time of battle, Friar Benigno patted me on the back and said, "That's enough now," and the situation calmed down. From that moment I understood what I had to do. I was completely convinced that God was with him; it could not have been otherwise. So then I told him that I had so many objects that I worked with, and after he explained to me what I had been doing, I promise to bring him everything. In spite of that, in the moment of surrendering him everything, I looked him in the eye and said: "Friar Benigno, it's not easy for someone like me to just throw all of this out and be freed of all of these things. Nonetheless, I want nothing to do with these things because now I understand my situation."

He continued to pray over me in a series of appointments, each one its own drama, and finally came to an end with my explicit renunciation of the power of command that I had. To be honest, I was involuntarily at the service of Satan for many years, without understanding the evil that I was doing to myself and others who had trusted me. I had become Satan's tool.

For the grace of God, for the love He has had for me, and thanks to Friar Benigno and his team members whom God used as instruments of his Church, and thanks to my own willpower to be freed, I was able to overcome a critical moment and confess my sins. Little by little, I put everything in its place and followed the regimen prescribed for me by those who belong to the "Listening Center". I also attended the five retreats of deliverance that focused on these kerygmatic statements:

- God loves you;
- Sin is at odds with the love of God;
- Jesus is the only Savior;
- Faith links you to the salvation that comes from Jesus;
- The Lordship of Jesus in your life;
- The Holy Spirit in your life.

Finally, I participated in the day-long conclusive retreat in which Friar Benigno prayed over us all en masse.

Now, I love have to go to Mass every day and the first thing I do when I get out of bed is take my Rosary in hand and begin to pray.

Given the experience I had, I can claim that Jesus is the only Savior and I cannot but affirm that only He is the Way, the Truth, and the Life.

One must eat in order to live. Analogously, if I do not nourish myself with Jesus I run the danger a falling into Satan's grip without being aware of it. I am convinced of this and that is why every day I allow myself to be nourished by the Body of Jesus, participating in the Holy Sacrifice of the Mass.

Part III

PUT ON THE ARMOR OF GOD
SO THAT YOU MAY BE ABLE TO STAND FIRM
AGAINST THE TACTICS OF THE DEVIL

(Eph 6:11)

Our battle against the powers of darkness

The Christian life and spiritual combat

After having presented testimonies from Fabio, Mario, Aurora, Marcella, Marianna, Teresa, Lorenzo, Sophia, Carol, Beatrice, Gertrude, Greta, Josie, and Jerry, all delivered through the intervention of the Lord, whose mercies know no end, we can say that diabolical activity, whether it be ordinary or extraordinary, has not finished yet. Consequently, we all have to fight every day against the devil, who *prowls about like a roaring lion looking for someone to devour* (1 Pet 5:8).

Our Christian life, therefore, is subject to battle. Indeed, we have a treasure to protect and to develop: that divine gift which was poured into us on the day of our baptism that makes us truly children of God, called to live with Him in a relationship of friendship and communion. This gift of grace will perdure perfectly after our death, when as children in the Son, living the very life of God, will be made similar to Him seeing him as he is (*cfr.* 1 Jn 3:1-2) and, enraptured by the Holy Spirit, we will be able to give ourselves totally to Him in a loving embrace that will bring us an eternal joy without measure. The devil, by way of this ordinary activity i.e., temptation, attempts to make us lose this treasure of divine life, and we are called to fight so that this not occur.

We must fight too, because we must resist the extraordinary activity of the devil, such as it is: infestation, obsession, oppression, and possession.

To be more precise, the battle in which we are engaged throughout our Christian life – as St. Paul tells us in *The Letter to the Ephesians,* is not in engagement with creatures of flesh and blood (cfr. Eph 6:12). The weapons we have in this battle are not of the flesh (cfr. 2 Cor 10:3). Thus, we use weapons of light (cfr. Rom 13:12), that come from God and are capable of destroying fortresses (cfr. 2 Cor 10:3-4).

St. Paul exhorted Timothy to fight the good fight (cfr. 1 Tim 1:18; 6:12), placing his hope in the living God (1 Tim 4:10). For his part, aware that he was about to pour out his own blood in libation and that the time was coming to extinguish his candle so as to enter life eternal, gave this testimony:

For I am already being poured out like a libation, and the time of my departure is at hand. I have competed well; I have finished the race; I have kept the faith. From now on the crown of righteousness awaits me, which the Lord, the just judge, will award to me on that day, and not only to me, but to all who have longed for his appearance (2 Tim 4:6-8).

Regarding this combat, the Vatican II document *Gaudium et Spes* affirms:

"For a monumental struggle against the powers of darkness pervades the whole history of man. The battle was joined from the very origins of the world and will continue until the last day, as the Lord has attested" (*GS* 37).

Further, *Lumen Gentium* exhorts the lay faithful to:

"....not hide this their hope then, in the depths of their hearts, but rather express it through the structure of their secular lives in continual conversion and in wrestling "against the world rulers of this darkness, against the spiritual forces of iniquity" (*LG* 35).

Already, at our origins, God pre-announced such a combat, when, after the sin of our first parents, he turned to the serpent, saying: *I will put enmity between you and the woman, and between your offspring and hers; He will strike at your head, while you strike at his heel.*

The descendancy of that woman who, crushed the head of the serpent in battle, is quite clearly Jesus Christ, but not only Jesus Christ, since He is the Head of a multitude who form His Mystical Body.

Thus, in the Proto-Evangelium, not only is combat foreseen, but also victory:

- Christ's battle as Head;
- The battle of those who form his Mystical Body.

Further, victory over the serpent is announced:

- Jesus Christ's victory as Head;
- As well as the victory of those members who have been joined to Him as branches to the vine.

In his earthly life as Son of Man, Christ engaged in an all out battle against the devil, winning a splendid victory: victory over temptation, victory through his exorcistic ministry, and, above all, victory through the Paschal mystery of his death and resurrection, which destroyed the work of the devil, becoming a pledge of both definitive and total victory to be completed at His second coming, when the devil will be bound forever and made incapable of doing us any more harm, be it through his ordinary activity or his extraordinary activity: he will be cast into the lake of fire in sulfur, where he will remain forever (cfr. Rev 19:20; 20;10).

As a result, after having reduced to nothing (in the order of power) every power and principality, that is the devil and his demons, so St. Paul tells us (cfr. 1 Cor 5:24), Jesus will hand over His kingdom to His Father. This will be the definitive victory, as the *Catechism of the Catholic Church* reminds us, will finally freeing all creation from corruption, sin, and death (*CCC* 2852).

Consequently, the battle of Jesus as Head becomes for us followers a mission to fulfill. Inasmuch as we are joined to Him as branches to the vine, we are called to fight the devil and his demons, whether it be on the field of his ordinary activity or that of his extraordinary activity, with the certainty that, in Him we too can share in his splendid victories. In this combat we distinguish a twofold strategy:

- A strategy of defense;
- A strategy of attack.

Strategy of defense combat against the devil

St. Paul writes:

> *Put on the armor of God so that you may be able to stand firm against the tactics of the devil. For our struggle is not with flesh and blood but with the principalities, with the powers, with the world rulers of this present darkness, with the evil spirits in the heavens. Therefore, put on the armor of God, that you may be able to resist on the evil day and, having done everything, to hold your ground. So stand fast with your loins girded in truth, clothed with righteousness as a breastplate, and your feet shod in readiness for the gospel of peace. In all circumstances, hold faith as a shield, to quench all (the) flaming arrows of the evil one. And take the helmet of salvation and the sword of the Spirit, which is the word of God. With all prayer and supplication, pray at every opportunity in the Spirit. To that end, be watchful with all perseverance and supplication for all the holy ones* (Eph 6:11-18).

In this passage, St. Paul describes for us how the spiritual life is made up of combat, which ought to be fought against the rulers of this present darkness, that is, against the evil spirits in the heavens (cfr. 6:12). For this battle one must be properly dressed, wearing an armor that reminds us of the Roman military uniform. But in our case this, it is God's armor (cfr. 6:11).

The Roman military gear took into account defensive as well as offensive means.

The defensive gear included:

- Loins girt (6:14);
- A breastplate (6:14);
- A shield (6:16)
- A helmet (6:17).
-

The offense of elements included:

- A sword for striking (6:17);
- And shod feet in order to better remove and, therefore, engage in battle with the enemy (6:15).

Furthermore, God's armor, similar to that of the Romans, according to Saint Paul, takes into account defensive measures can means of attack against the rulers of this world of darkness.

The means of defense are:

- Truth (6:14);
- Justice (6:14)
- Faith (6:16)
- Salvation (6:17).

The means of attacking the rulers of this world are:

- The Word of God (6:17)
- Zeal and readiness proclaim the Gospel of peace (6:15).

Finally, the divine weaponry used to fight the rulers of this world of darkness include:

- Constant prayer (6:18);

- Vigilance (6:18);
- Perseverance (6:18);
- Intercession for our brothers and sisters (6:18), so that they two, in defending themselves against evil spirits and in attacking them, may come out victorious.

To those means proposed to us by St. Paul, we can add others that defend us against the devil and help us to avoid those attacks that result from his extraordinary activity such as possession, oppression, obsession, and infestation, by not opening up certain doors:

- Membership in Satanic sects;
- Participation in Satanic rituals, in particular, the so-called "black mass";
- A consecration to Satan (former Satanists have brought me the formal text of this consecration for my perusal);
- A pact made with Satan (many of the people who have come to me seeking exorcisms have made such pacts);
- Participation in séances;
- Visiting sorcerers, palm readers, tarot card readers, psychics, healers, *curanderos,* et al. (here I am referring to those who have received certain powers from Satan, not necessarily to those charlatans who profit from psychologically weak people, taking advantage of them and fleecing them of their money. Of course, even in this case, it constitutes a grave sin against the first commandment, but normally does not open a door to the extraordinary action of the devil);
- Contact with people who claim to have "spirit guides" or "good spirits" who help them;
- Listening to satanic rock music whose message is an invitation to the cult of Satan, to violence, to necrophilia, and to suicide;
- The use of amulets and talismans that have been cursed by sorcerers;

- The practice of automatic writing, card reading, palm reading, and magic;
- Seeking out a medium to invoke the spirits of the dead and similar practices.

Moreover, we can add something else that defends us against the devil and helps us to avoid those attacks that result from his extraordinary activity such as possession, oppression, obsession, and infestation: by living constantly in the state of grace. Pope Pius VI teaches us: "Everything that defends us from sin strengthens us by that very fact against the invisible enemy. Grace is the decisive defense. Innocence takes on the aspect of strength".[11]

God's grace is the decisive defense against the invisible enemy precisely because living in grace implies a life lived in profound intimacy with God. Further, when such friendship becomes loving obedience, it is fed by the Word of God, nourished by the Eucharist, restored by the sacrament of reconciliation, and receives continual support from the other sacraments and personal prayer, such friendship constitutes the armor of God, that St. Paul counsels for resistance of the devil's deceits (Eph 6:11).

This principle should be clear: the more a man lives in friendship with God, so much less can the devil and his subordinates demons achieve to overcome him through temptation. Furthermore, excluding those exceptional cases which form part of God's mysterious and loving design, the more a man lives in friendship with God, so much less is the devil table to attack him through possession, oppression, obsession, and infestation.

---

[11] General Audience, November 15, 1972.

Strategy of the fence regarding evil thoughts caused by the devil

The origins of evil thoughts

According to the Church Fathers, the origins of evil thoughts are three:

- They can be engendered by our dispositions;
- They can be engendered by our predispositions;
- They can be engendered by demonic activity.

1. Dispositions are made up of those passions present within us, which present themselves primarily by way of our thoughts.

2. Predispositions, on the other hand, are made up of those memories of past wounds, that have left their marks upon us. Thus, beyond those evil thoughts that are actually voluntary, we also find involuntary thoughts, that are fruit of one's voluntary thoughts. As a result, they are involuntary consequences whose cause, at one time, was voluntary.

3. The last source of evil thoughts is demonic activity. Demons can bring about passionate thoughts within us, using our weaknesses, and taking into account our dispositions and our predispositions. In each of these cases, the devil uses our memory and our imagination to arouse within us passionate and visceral thought. In these cases we are often induced to think that these particular passions proceed from our hearts, when in truth they have been provoked exclusively by demons.

The stages of temptation

1. The first stage of temptation is known as "suggestion" or "attack". In this case, it regards an evil thought, or better said, an evil image of something that suddenly sprouts up within our heart without our will giving any consent. In this first phase, not having engendered the thought or the consent freely, it does not constitute a sin. In the beginning, this was what happened to Eve, when she was tempted by the devil in the form of the serpent: *Now the serpent was the most cunning of all the animals that the LORD God had made. The serpent asked the woman, "Did God really tell you not to eat from any of the trees in the garden?"* (Gen 3:1).

2. The second stage of temptation involves a relationship. There are two steps but make up this relationship: the first is made up of a simple interior conversation that we may have with the evil thought. In this conversation, we stop and discuss back and forth with the evil thought, *sans* the passions; that is, without, properly speaking, binding ourselves to it. In this case no sin is involved, inasmuch as we have not consented to the evil thought, merely discussed with it: *The woman answered the serpent: "We may eat of the fruit of the trees in the garden; it is only about the fruit of the tree in the middle of the garden that God said, 'You shall not eat it or even touch it, lest you die.'" But the serpent said to the woman: "You certainly will not die!* (Gen 3:2-4).

The second step takes place when we enter in a relational way with the evil spirit, seeing it as desirable, beautiful, pleasurable, without giving full consent. In this case there is a sin, but not mortal: *But the serpent said to the woman: "You certainly will not die! No, God knows well that the moment you eat of it your eyes will be opened and you will be like gods who know what is good and what is bad." The woman saw that the tree was good for food, pleasing to the eyes, and desirable for gaining wisdom* (Gen 3:4-6a).

3. The third stage of temptation is constituted of consent. It involves intellectual assent accompanied by a certain delight. And so it is in the field of the thoughts that we commit the sin, having given our full consent to that which was proposed to us, having accepted the pleasure of the thought and having acted upon it, abandoning ourselves to the pleasure the thought provides us.

4. The fourth stage of temptation is made up of what is called "slavery." Having given for consent of thought, we become slaves to it: *He who commits a sin,* says Jesus, *becomes a slave of sin* (Jn 8:34).

5. The fifth stage of temptation is made up of its consummation, "the act itself" of the passionate thought to which we consented. In other words, having given assent to the thought we have become prisoners of it, and then we move to carrying out the sin in act: *So she took some of its fruit and ate it; and she also gave some to her husband, who was with her, and he ate it* (Gen 3:6b).

6. The sixth stage of temptation is made up of the "passion" as repetition of our consent to a thought of a similar sort, bringing about corresponding passions; that is, reinforcing the passion that has already taken root within us.

How can we defend ourselves against temptations caused by the Devil?

Before answering this question it is important to remember that no one is spared ordinary diabolical activity in the form of temptations. That is why, even the great saints, such as St. Francis of Assisi (cfr. *FF* 702), who have achieved a degree of impassibility and obtained the purification of their past faults from which are no longer engendered dispositions nor predispositions, are still confronted at times by those thoughts produced by demons, constituting, for them, temptations.

Indeed, according to the Fathers, diabolical activity multiplies, along with the accompanying evil thoughts, in the measure of one's spiritual progress. Hesychius of Sinai teaches us: "just as it is impossible to walk this earth without breathing in air, so too, it is impossible that the heart of man not be continually attacked by demons or secretly tormented by them."[12]

The path demons follow to arouse evil thoughts within us involves increasing than us the role of the passions, thus pushing us towards sins of action, or simply to make us turn within ourselves, to those passions from which.

This takes another shape, however, in the form of disturbing the prayer of one who has been delivered from the power of the passions, by impeding him from achieving the heights of contemplation.

---

[12] *Chapters on Vigilance,* 114.

Whatever the case, demons do whatever they can to distance us from God and turn us against Him.

With this in mind, evil thoughts presented by demons, appear as temptations, leaving us two options:

- To accept them, carrying out will of the devil,
- Or to reject it, doing the will of God.

Thus, every evil thought that presents itself to us comes in the form of a test that leads us:

- To our eternal damnation;
- or to our salvation, depending on the choice we make.

Furthermore, giving into temptation, we perpetuate within ourselves a state of sin and set ourselves up further falls. If, however, we do not give in, we can heal past wounds and avoid further spiritual damage.

St. James underlines the positive function of temptations: *Blessed is the man who perseveres in temptation, for when he has been proved he will receive the crown of life that he promised to those who love him* (Jm 1:12).

Thus, our attitude confronting evil thoughts determines our spiritual destiny. It is by means of consent to thoughts that passions are born and persist, and demons take possession of the soul, residing in its vicinity. On the contrary, by rejection of those thoughts, carried out with the help of God, we can be delivered from our passions and progress in virtue, uniting ourselves to God in that union.

A) *Be sober and vigilant* (1 Pet 5:8)

A proper strategy of defense in combating evil thoughts and overcoming demonic attacks must include vigilance. The recommendation to remain sober individual and is found frequently throughout Jesus' discourses:

- *Be alert..... Watch... What I tell you, I tell everyone: be vigilant* (Mk 13:33,35,37);
- *Blessed those servants whom the master, upon his return, finds awake; in truth I tell you, he will gird up his garments, seat them at table and serve them* (Lk 12:37-38);
- *Be vigilant at all times and pray that you have the strength to escape the tribulations that are imminent and to stand before the Son of Man* (Lk 21:36);
- *He said to them: my soul is sorrowful unto death. Stay here and watch* (Mk 14:34);
- *Watch and pray that you not fall into temptation. The spirit is willing, but the flesh is weak* (Mk 14:38).

In the writings of St. Paul, too, we find similar counsels to vigilance: *let us not sleep like the others, but the vigilant and sober* (1 Thess 5:6);

Similarly, St. Peter writes: *be sober and vigilant. Your enemy, the devil, prowls about like a roaring lion looking for someone to devour. Resist him, steadfast in the faith* (1 Pet 5:8).

To be sober and watchful with regard to ourselves means, to have a general vigilance over ourselves, being concerned in the first place with our spiritual destiny much more than for exterior things. Thus watchful of our external behavior, we avoid evil actions.

Nonetheless, as we have seen, it is precisely from thoughts that actions are engendered, the birth and cultivation of passions depends on our thoughts and it is precisely here, above all, where we should direct our vigilant attention. Indeed, from such vigilance depends our victory, inasmuch as vigilance and watchfulness, functions as our greatest support in spiritual combat.

To be sober and watchful with regard to our thoughts means a continual custody of our heart so that we can observe the thoughts that are born there and, in due time, defend ourselves from the sudden and unforeseen attacks of the enemy.

To be sober and watchful with regard to our thoughts means, ultimately, examining each thought to determine its origin, in order to recognize its nature, to see if it is a good, indifferent, or evil thought. This means an attitude of discernment of thoughts.

In order for sobriety and vigilance to be fully effective, they must be constant, without ceasing.

After due discernment, and according to the nature of the thoughts, one ought to adopt, according to each case, the corresponding response:

- If it involves a good or different thoughts, one may entertain it because it will not bring with that negative consequences, except in case of when it occurs during prayer, thus taking the form of a distraction, a hindrance to union.

- Not so with evil thoughts. One must always and absolutely avoid cultivation also slots, rejecting them as soon as they arise, as we have seen described in the stage of consent.

To reject people thoughts there are two methods to adopt:

- The first involves considering the thought and entering into discussion with it, without giving consent. Here, what is involved in this discussion with the thought is how to contradict it, to refute it, opposing it with varied arguments from Scripture, as Christ did in his temptations (cfr Mt 4:1-10). Such a method of combating evil thoughts ought to be reserved, so say Fathers, to those who are sufficiently advanced in the spiritual life, knowing how not to allow oneself to be seduced by the enemy's arguments, as Eve was (Gen 3:1-6). Certainly, even for the perfect, entering into discussion with evil thoughts to combat them presents a very real risk, as it may develop into suggestion, bringing with it a certain inner turbation, or even any interest in that thought, resulting in damage to one's vigilance, weakening one's prayer. In a certain sense, one becomes the enemy's plaything.

- The second method to adopt – the one preferred by the Fathers – regards a refusal to allow the thought entry into one's heart, rejecting it at its birth, so that put to death in its nascent form, all discussion is avoided and there is no need to argue with it and contradict it.

B) *Pray without ceasing*

Along with sobriety and vigilance, the strategy to overcome demonic attacks of evil thoughts requires prayer, which plays an indispensable and constitutes the principal arm of defense at our disposal. Christ himself associates one with the other: *Watch and pray so that you do not fall into temptation* (Mt 26:41).

The fight against evil thoughts is, therefore, a long-term operation, whose total victory requires much time and dedication. During this period, discouragement is a constant threat. In order to overcome it, we have to bring to mind the words of St. James already cited: *Blessed is the man who perseveres in temptation, for when he has been proved he will receive the crown of life that he promised to those who love him* (Jm 1:12). Christ himself says: *He who perseveres to the end will be saved* (Mt 10:22).

The strategy of attack in combat against the Devil

Is not enough to merely defend ourselves in the fight against the devil and his demons. Defense is efficient, but not sufficient. We need, moreover, a strategy of attack, cooperating with Jesus Christ to destroy the works of the devil, announcing the Gospel of peace, carrying out apostolate, shaping Christian society, and sometimes, exorcism. Let us consider each one of these points.

Cooperating with Jesus to destroy the works of the devil

We actively fight against the devil and his demons, participating in the victories of Jesus Christ in the following ways:

- Every effort we make it to eliminate within ourselves the work of the devil, that is, sin;
- Every time, by way of our apostolate, we help others break with sin and live in friendship with God the Father, by bringing them from the kingdom of darkness to the Kingdom of Light, to live as children in communion with their heavenly Father;

- Whenever we suffer, be it from natural causes or from the hand of the Evil One, we unite ourselves to the power of the death and resurrection of Jesus Christ, and we bring others to participate in that same power through the love that we offer God in our suffering. Suffering, by the way, entered by way of sin, but in this case it becomes something that sanctifies us and others. Through such an offering, we grow in holiness and receive in return an eternal and immeasurable degree of glory (cfr 2 Cor 4:17), fulfilling what was lacking in the suffering of Christ, making up for it in our own flesh for the salvation of the world (Col 1:24). Hence, the Cross – as Pope Francis says – becomes the theological place of our victory.[13]

Announcing the Gospel of peace

We offensively attack the devil and his demons, participating in the victories of Jesus Christ:

Each time, as workers in the vineyard, we toil in preaching the Gospel of peace (Eph 6:15), teaching the men of our time that they are loved by God. In fact, when the Word of God penetrates the heart of man, it acts like rainfall, *For just as from the heavens the rain and snow come down and do not return there till they have watered the earth, making it fertile and fruitful, Giving seed to him who sows and bread to him who eats, so shall my word be that goes forth from my mouth; It shall not return to me void, but shall do my will, achieving the end for which I sent it* (Is 55:10-11).

---

[13] *Aprite la mente al cuore,* ed. Rizzoli, 2013, p.64.

Carrying out apostolate

We positively attack the devil and his demons, participating in the victories of Christ:

- Every time, as workers in the Vineyard of the Lord, we live the gospel serving others in order that they discover their own inviolable dignity as human persons, the defending and respecting (and bringing others to do the same) the right to life and the right to religious freedom.

Shaping Christian society

Every time that we, as workers in the Vineyard of the Lord, live the gospel and serve society, not just on an individual level, but on the level of society, we shaped correctly:

- Through promotion of the family;
- Through carrying out corporal and spiritual works of mercy towards our neighbor, using old and new methods;
- Awakening our brothers to the faith so as to direct politics and shaped the Christian society;
- Making the workplace a community of respect (within the natural law) of each individual;
- Carrying out works and apostolates, and bringing others to do so with professionalism, honesty, and Christian spirit as a way of personal sanctification;
- Dedicating ourselves to the evangelization of the culture;
- And bringing about an atmosphere that lets the social economic structure serve the person, and not the other way around.

Every time we live the Gospel shaping a Christian society and all of these forms, we positively and effectively fight the powers of darkness in this world, sharing in the victories of Christ

We have the possibility of participating in a still greater victory over the devil in our last battle against him, which will take place in the moment of our death. Death entered into the world through the temptation our first parents underwent in which the devil came out victorious. But if we allow ourselves, one more time, to participate in the power of the death and resurrection of Jesus Christ and are thus capable to offer our death with love to the Father in union with the death of His beloved Son for the salvation of the world, this will be for us our last and greatest victory over the devil.

To exorcise, following certain rules

Finally, we have the strategy of attack against the powers of this world, that, in rare cases (fortunately!) torment the children of God through possession, oppression, obsession, and infestation, with the weapon of the solemn or great exorcism. This, nonetheless, must be used strictly following certain rules, applying them *servatis servandis,* to simple prayers of healing and deliverance that priests and lay faithful may use.

1. It is worth mentioning to the lay faithful and priests, who are not exorcists, that it is not licit for them to carry out the liturgical solemn exorcism, neither In the invocative nor imperative form[14]. Nor is it licit for them to use a non-liturgical exorcism, that is, a private exorcism, in which commands are given.[15] Finally, it is not licit to use the

---

[14] *Code of Canon Law,* 1172, 1.

[15] *Letter to Ordinaries regarding Norms on Exorcisms,* CDF, September 24, 1985.

integral form of the formula of the exorcism against Satan and the rebellious angels published by Pope Leo the XIII, since it is reserved, by norm of the rite, to those who have been mandated to use the solemn form of exorcism.

2. It is, nonetheless, licit for a priest who is not the exorcist to lead a community in prayers of deliverance using appendix I of the new rite of exorcism, excluding, however, the exorcistic formulae contained there. In such encounters, everything must be done to avoid every sort of abuse and ambiguity, making reference to the directive from the Congregation for the Doctrine of Faith in its *Instruction on Prayers of Healing* of September 14, 2000, which excludes the use of such prayers within the celebration of the Holy Mass, the sacraments, and the Liturgy of the Hours.[16]

3. It is licit however for every faithful, to pray non-liturgical prayers to obtain healing.[17] When such prayers are carried out in the community, in a church, or in a sacred space, they are to be led by an ordained priest,[18] insuring, that, especially those who lead them do not fall into any form of hysteria, theatrics, simulation, or sensationalism, carrying them out with serene devotion.[19] Such prayers, be they non-liturgical or liturgical, may only be carried out with the explicit permission of the diocesan Bishop,[20] and ought to remain distinct from the prayers of exorcism

---

[16] *Enchiridion Vatincanum,* 19, n. 1290.

[17] Congregation for the Doctrine of Faith in its *Instruction on Prayers of Healing* of September 14, 2000, art. 1.

[18] *O.c.,* art. 1.

[19] *EV,* 19, n. 1288.

[20] *EV,* 19, 1287.

contained in the official rite of exorcism,[21] nor may they be introduced into the celebration of the Holy Eucharist, the sacraments, or the Liturgy of the Hours, with the exception that such petitions for the faithful that have been previously included in the prayers of the faithful. In that case, one may offer prayer intentions for the healing of the sick.[22]

4. A priest who his not an exorcist or a layman, who would offer a prayer of healing or deliverance for an individual in a non-liturgical setting, may use to this end a psalm, an appropriate Gospel passage, the *Our Father,* or other prayers, preferably those that come from Church Tradition.

5. The exorcist:
- Ought to have a thorough knowledge of the *Praenotandae* of the rite of exorcism;
- Observe the Church's norms in carrying out the exorcism;
- Care for his own spiritual life, striving for holiness;
- Be dedicated in his own specific formation, initial and permanent, living out in all of their dimensions – especially in the areas of penance and contemplation – involving other people in this work to obtain the deliverance of the people who turned to him for help;
- Avoid putting their faith in techniques to obtain deliverance, but exercise more directly, Faith in Jesus Christ, the only one who can bring about deliverance;
- Adhere to the text of the ritual, but also having recourse to prayers approved by the Church after having concluded the exorcism and before proceeding to the

---

[21] *EV*, 19, n. 1290.

[22] *EV*, 19, 1290.

repetition of the prayers provided in the rite of exorcisms.

6. Proper to the liturgical action of exorcism, he ought to avoid all expressions of hysteria or unhealthy curiosity, so that the exorcism not become a spectacle and out of respect for the person who is tormented by the Evil One. During the prayer of exorcism all means of social communication are prohibited for use by the exorcist himself or those who participate in the exorcism (or before and after it), avoiding divulgence of what occurs, maintaining a just reserve.[23] It is fitting to add, out of respect for the person tormented by the Evil One, one ought to avoid picture taking or videos, even if only for private use.

7. Regarding prayers done over women, whether by an exorcist, a priest who is not an exorcist, or lay faithful:
   - They should refrain from laying their hands on any part of the body;
   - They should avoid anything that would call into question their chastity, even though their intentions be correct;
   - Avoid telling the person that he has been the object of the curse and, especially, never indicate who made the curse;
   - They should remember that this fight against the devil takes place on the spiritual plane, not the physical one; therefore, they should abstain from any violent behavior with regard to people who are victims of the extraordinary activity of the devil, such as pulling their hair, slapping them, kicking them, or strapping them down, thinking to humiliate the devil in this way.

---

[23] *Praenotandae*, 19.

8. Ordinarily, and for various reasons, the exorcist ought to be accompanied by a group of people, even if very few, during the rite of exorcism.

9. In order to avoid that the exorcism become a spectacle for those are present, the exorcist ought to ensure that amongst those present who participate, no one is there out of curiosity.

10. Recognizing the clear distinction between those authentic gifts of the Holy Spirit and those of the so-called "sensitives", that is, those people who have powers that come from the Evil One, exorcists, priests who are not exorcists, and lay faithful ought to carry out prayers of deliverance, of healing, and exorcism with this distinction in mind.

11. Exorcisms, prayers of deliverance, and prayers of healing ought be carried out in a way that manifests the faith of the Church, ensuring that these are not interpreted as magical or superstitious acts[24]. As a result, exorcists, priests who are not exorcists, and the lay faithful:

*   Do not attribute an automatic efficacy to the gestures they employ – even liturgically – since that mentality belongs to the world of magic, not faith.
*   They should avoid gestures not prescribed by the liturgy, or anything ambiguous that could be interpreted as a magical gesture;
*   They should avoid engendering in the faithful the conviction that their deliverance or healing will only

---

[24] *Praenotandae* 19.

come about if he executes certain gestures or says a particular precise number of prayers or uses holy water in a special way. Such attitudes reveal a magical mentality

- They should be vigilant with regard to the faith of the faithful who turn to them for help: it is not an authentic expression of faith to request holy water, blessed oil, less salt, when one habitually misses Sunday Mass, Holy Communion, and confession. In such a case, the use of sacramentals are reduced to magical objects; therefore this must be avoided.

12. It is necessary that the entire pastoral activity of exorcism in prayers of deliverance and healing are separate and unbound to the offerings of money, obliging the afflicted to pay a fee. The refusal of free will offerings is also suggested to avoid the impression of the monetary exchange used by sorcerers, putting into practice the words of the Lord: *What you have received freely, give freely.*

13. The exorcist, beyond being very particular about the lay faithful he chooses to work with him, ought to ensure that these are people of prayer, faith, morally integral people. He ought to instruct them about what they may do and may not do, and that their presence ought to be subject to every sign of humility and discretion. Furthermore, they ought to be vigilant that they not adopt the posture of protagonist, seeking to take the place of the exorcist in discernment, especially during the moment of exorcism itself; nor should they substitute him in the spiritual direction of the possessed faithful.

14. Those qualified to be admitted to the exorcism may intervene through their own private prayer, done in the silence of their hearts, or participating in the prayers of the rite of exorcism as prescribed in the ritual through their vocal responses. It is strictly forbidden for them to repeat the exorcistic formula, in this liturgical form or private, non-liturgical form – something that is reserved to the exorcist alone.

Such are the rules that exorcists ought to observe in the use of the weapon of the solemn exorcism that the Church has received from the Lord. And, in their turn, *servatis servandis*, priests were not exorcists and lay faithful ought to limit themselves two simple prayers of healing and deliverance.

We conclude this chapter, returning to the theme of spiritual combat. We must admit that this is truly difficult. We have around us, but also within us, so many enemies who fight us, enemies who are quite strong: not just the devil and his angels, but as well our own concupiscence of the flesh, the concupiscence of the eyes, and the pride of life. We also are in the midst of a world with its structures of sin created by us, and nonetheless, fighting against us.

How are we to confront all of this we are so weak?

We may not permit fear of any sort. If, in fact, it is true that the battle is hard and if it is true that we are truly weak, it is just as true that Jesus Christ is with us: *Go forth, teach all nations.... Behold I am with you every day until the end of the world* (Mt 28:20).

If, in our weakness, we should fall, and as long as there are no impediments, Jesus, who is with us, will come to us in his mercy. That is the true medicine that has the power to heal so many wounds, many of which suffered in our own fight. Therefore, there is no place for fear: *Fear not,* says Jesus, *I have overcome the world.*

"Perfection," so says St. Francis de Sales, "does not consist in the absence of perfections, but in the effort to combat them."

Enzo Bianchi writes:

> The Christian life is not a continual ascent to the heights after a definitive victory against sin; rather a constant return to beg of God's mercy, falling, and getting up again without end; this is the incessant art of starting anew one's conformity with Christ, it requires having constant recourse to the chalice of His Blood that purifies and pardon's our sins.[25]

The Lord, therefore, does not ask us to not suffer wounds in our spiritual combat, but He does ask us to never surrender and to persevere in our constant battle. What we cannot attain of our own effort, He supplies in His mercy.

---

[25] *Resisti al nemico. La lotta spiritual,* p. 42.

Part IV

The Exorcistic Ministry

Pastoral thoughts and recollections

To end this book, I decided to use this last chapter to lay out some pastoral indications for the exercise of this ministry, along with some personal recollections.

Caution and prudence necessary for this ministry:

Praenotandae 14 says that the exorcist ought to be distinguished for his caution and prudence, and is warned by the Church not to fall into credulity with each encounter of persons claiming to be possessed by demons. Such cases are often, sadly, cases of illness, above all those of a psychological nature, or fruit of one's imagination.

This reminds me of a young man who came to me. He had been receiving prayers of deliverance from a priest, who thought he diagnosed a diabolical possession. I followed the case for a while, using some prayers.

One day his parish priest brought him to me. We spoke at length. Three elements emerged from that conversation: upon entering the church: he would immediately want to leave; when walking up to receive Communion he would begin to laugh; and when St. Gemma Galgani was mentioned – so he said – the demons within him were unleashed. These are the three elements that made him think but he was dealing with a spiritual disturbance of a demonic nature. But there was something that didn't leave me convinced.

I had him sit down in the room where I do the exorcisms and there, we witnessed the scene that would make one think that this was a case of the spiritual disturbance. He took a chair and threw it in the air and began to blaspheme the Lord in a horrible way. I still wasn't convinced.

I got him to sit down again and, without him noticing it, touched his back with a relic of St. Gemma that I had my pocket. No reaction. "How strange," I thought to myself. But upon mentioning St. Gemma, the demons came unleashed. Approaching him, with the relic of the saint provoked no reaction.

At this point I changed the strategy. I told him that I would pray silently, and so began. The reactions were very violent. A second time I repeated the same prayer. Reactions again. I asked the priest who accompanied him to join me in prayer, reciting the prayer we had on a paper in our hands silently. "The prayer of two," I explained, "has a greater efficacy." The reactions were more violent.

Then I approached that young man, telling him: "There's nothing wrong with you. Do you know what prayer we said? Here it is: *Lord Jesus, please let this pseudo-prayer which I am about to do be used as an instrument of discernment: 'Aunt Concetta is under the fig tree playing with Aunt Lucia.'* Calm down. You're not possessed." With that, his facial muscles relaxed, he began to look serene and relieved. So I suggested he visit to psychiatrist.

But then the question arose: "If I am mistaken in my discernment, what of the psychiatrist fills with medicines bringing about negative consequences, and all of the side effects?"

So, I called the parish priests, asking him to bless a bottle of water and put it in the sacristy on the counter. "The next time you see him, offer him a drink and let me know how he reacts."

Response: "No reaction."

Furthermore, everything is going back to normal – so he told me – since he saw me last: he participates in Mass without any difficulty and the accompanying disturbances have all disappeared. So what happened here? The forensic psychopathologist on my team explained to me that such a phenomenon is not unknown in psychiatry. When one is convinced of something, particularly that one is possessed, the unconscious mind imposes gestures proper to possession to convince oneself and others that this is, indeed, a case of possession. The priest, who had done the diagnosis of a diabolical possession and continued with prayers of deliverance to free him, had conditioned him.

Consequently, the Church is correct in inviting the exorcist to not fall into credulity before every person claiming to be possessed by the devil, since it could be the case of an ill person, especially a psychologically unstable person or fruit of one's imagination.[26]

Knowing how to distinguish

Number 15 of the *Praenotandae* tells us that the exorcist is enjoined by the Church to distinguish well between cases of diabolical aggression and those born of a certain credulity that makes some people believe themselves to be the object of spells and curses, bringing misfortune to them, their family members, and their property.

I remember the phone call from a certain woman.

"Friar Beningo, I have urgent need of an exorcism."

"What's going on? Tell me."

"Just give me an appointment and I'll tell you face-to-face."

"Excuse me, Ma'am, just tell me what's going on."

"Well here it is: I have been separated for my husband for six years now. And in all of this time I have not been able to find a man with whom I can form a new family. Clearly somebody has cursed me and I ask you to do an exorcism over me as soon as possible."

---

[26] Cfr *Praenotandae* 1.

"Ma'am, hear me out," I said with a degree of irony – "I'm rather competent in this area. This is not a curse. Rather, it is the grace of God and let us hope that you never find this new man."

That woman, mistakenly convinced that she was the victim of a curse and wanted me to do an exorcism over her so that she would find a man with whom to form a family, with the consequence of beginning a new life of sin!

Another woman called asking urgently for an appointment for an exorcism because of her conviction that she too was the object of a curse. For the last six years – so she said – she has been separated from her husband and lived with another man with whom she wanted to have children. She wanted to have children with this other man and couldn't. Surely, she was under a curse and I had to do an exorcism for her so that, once delivered, she might have children with a man who is not her husband. Incredible....

One day somebody called me saying: "I have an urgent need of an exorcism. I'm requesting an appointment as early as possible."

"Tell me what's going on."

"I'm unemployed and can't find work. Most certainly somebody has cursed me."

I responded, "Bring me all of the unemployed of Palermo and then make me understand why only you are cursed and not the others."

A certain facility to believe oneself demonically disturbed is a reality. We understand why the Church exhorts exorcists to distinguish well those cases of diabolical aggression and those that derive from credulity, inducing people to believe themselves the object of curses and spells affecting them, the families, and their goods.[27]

THE INVOCATIVE EXORCISM AND ITS VALUE

It must be said that manifestations of psychological pathology and diabolical manifestations are very similar, and at times, even for those who are competent, it can be extremely difficult to discern, given the similarity, but also because the those revealing elements of extraordinary diabolical activity are not always clear.

In these cases, the invocactive form of the exorcism can be of great help, which serves also as a diagnostic tool which, during the invocative exorcism, can make certain elements appear that aid the exorcist in his discernment.

I remember a young man who came to me, sent by the Capuchin Fathers of Castelvetrano, who had diagnosed in him a diabolical possession. I had a long interview with him, but it seemed to me that some of the elements were lacking in him that would give evidence of a diabolical possession. I sighed within myself, "Some people see the Devil everywhere..." so I asked him if he went confession.

"I never confess," he said, "because I don't believe in anything."

"Well, if you do not believe in anything," I responded, "I can do nothing for you."

---

[27] Cfr *Praenotandae* 15,

I called his father who was waiting in the other room and told him that I could do nothing for his son because he didn't believe in anything. He broke out crying, "No, Father, my son believes."

I was so moved by his tears that I understood that I could not release the boy to his father so quickly. I seated his son in the room where I do exorcisms and I began to do the Litany of the Saints. Immediately his son entered into a trance and manifested the typical signs of a diabolical possession. Consequently, I proceeded with the exorcism in its invocative form followed by the imperative. When he came back to himself I asked him, "So do you believe in the Lord Jesus Christ?"

"Of course, I believe," was his ready response.

"Do you want to go to confession?"

"Most definitely, Father, it's been a while."

Clearly, the devil was well hidden. He was hidden in the affirmation of atheism and the declaration of refusal to confess his sins. But with prayer, the Devil was unmasked and, above all during the prayer of exorcism, forced to manifest himself.

THE POSITIVE EFFECTS AFTER THE INVOCATIVE EXORCISM AND ITS DIAGNOSITCAL VALUE

Some elements may not manifest themselves during the invocative form of exorcism, and nonetheless, have a certain explorative and diagnostic value with regard to the positive effects that they bring about later. The same thing here can also happen to a doctor who, not having all of the elements for a clear diagnosis and limiting himself to speculation about the certain illness, prescribes a determined therapy. If this brings about the good results *ex adiuvantibus* – using the medical jargon – the previous hypotheses is confirmed and the therapy continued to bring about the full recovery.

I remember, in this regard what happened to a certain young couple. They had been married for five years and during those five years were incapable of having conjugal relations. Was this a psychological problem? I thought I would try some pointed questions. I said, "At this point I am not asking about a moral problem. But I need to ask you some questions which will help me understand the situation."

"Before you were married where you engaged?"

"Yes."

"How long were you engaged before your marriage?"

"For three years."

"During those three years did you have sexual relations?"

"Yes."

"With difficulties?"

"No."

"With no difficulties whatsoever?"

"With no difficulties."

"When did the problems begin?"

"The night of our wedding. Ever since then we have been unable to have relations.

From the responses I began to believe that there might be a curse on their marriage. It was a hypothesis that I formulated interiorly. Thus, I began the invocative form of the exorcism. There were no reactions. Nonetheless, after a few days they called me up, telling me that everything was fine. In this case, the positive effects of the exorcism confirmed the hypothesis I formulated. There was a diabolical oppression, most likely caused by curse.

When an exorcist is limited to formulating a hypothesis of possession or some sort of vexation, before sending him to a psychiatrist who will fill him with pills, an invocative exorcism can be a help.

A PRAYERFUL AND PENITENTIAL CHURCH BEHIND THE EXORCIST

If an exorcist is not backed up by a prayerful and penitent Church, the time of liberation can be retarded. If, on the other hand, he reckons with a prayerful and penitential Church, the deliverance comes more easily.

This statement has been confirmed when my superior called together all of the faithful who attend our Sunday Mass – some 700 people – asking them to pray the Rosary every day for the people who come to me to receive exorcisms. 700 rosaries every day.

I was full of wonder and gratitude towards the Lord considering that He, with all of those Rosaries that are a repeated intercession of his Mother to Him, should have brought about the definitive deliverance of some 50 people that year.

Another confirmation. Participating in the International Association of Exorcists conference in 2,000, I was impressed by an African exorcist who, speaking to us European exorcists, said with great simplicity: "I don't understand you. In order to bring somebody to definitive deliverance it takes you years of prayer and exorcism!?! I pray the exorcism prayers once and always achieve definitive deliverance."

"Blessed are you!", Exclaimed Father Gabriele Amorth. "In my best of cases, I have to see someone weekly for two years to achieve definitive deliverance."

Later, we understood why that African exorcist required only one exorcism to arrive at deliverance. His parish was as big as a medium-sized diocese. He involves all of his parishioners in a prayer chain that went round-the-clock every day. They prayed night and day for the deliverance of those people, victims of extraordinary diabolical action that he worked with in his ministry. Hence, the simple explanation for his success after only one exorcism.

THE EXORCISM OF NON-CHRISTIANS

Exorcism can bringing non-Christians to faith in Jesus Christ in the moment in which they experience that *there is no salvation through anyone else, nor is there any other name under heaven given to the human race by which we are to be saved* (Acts 4:12). In this case, exorcism becomes an opportunity for evangelization and proclamation of the faith.

I remember, in this regard, that a Muslim girl of 17 years, accompanied by her Catholic social worker who had noticed in her signs that aroused suspicion of diabolical possession. I was not able to proceed with the exorcism without informing the Bishop of the diocese as the norms of the Church establish (*Praenotandae* 18). But before doing so, I proclaimed before her the *Prologue* of John's Gospel. Immediately, the girl entered into a trance and began to writhe about violently. The reactions and increased when, after proclaiming that Gospel passage, I began to pray the *Salve Regina*. It was clear that this was a case of diabolical possession.

Therefore, I went to the bishop to inform him so that he would authorize me to exercise that girl.

"But what sense does an exorcism have for and unbaptized girl?" he objected. He continued, "Either exorcism is in function of baptism about to be received or for the person already baptized."

And so I answered his objection saying, "Your Excellency," I said smiling, "the norm tells me to inform the Bishop of the diocese, which is what I am doing right now, as you can see. It doesn't tell me not to do the exorcism."

He looked at me and, smiling as well, added, "Fine, just do it."

I intuited that the Lord would grant that girl her deliverance, giving her in, that way, a sign of the truth of our religion, helping her to convert.

After receiving the proper consent from her legal guardians, I began the exorcistic therapy. After only seven exorcisms the girl was delivered, totally and definitively.

"Aziz," I said to her. "I was not the one who delivered you. You were delivered by Jesus Christ, who died in the Cross for me and for you. Say to Jesus: "Jesus, thank you for what you have done for me."

"Jesus, thank you for what you have done for me," she said. Imagine a Muslim praying like that. Then, she told me, "I'm going to become Catholic. I'm so afraid they'll kill me."

IS IT RECOMMENDED THAT THOS AFFLICTED BY THE DEVIL ATTEND COMMUNITY PRAYER MEETINGS?

For those who exercise the ministry of exorcism, I think my experience might be useful.

I think it is to be discouraged for people afflicted with spiritual problems of a demonic nature to participate in community prayer meetings, where often other people are present with the same problem. What follows are the motivations for this affirmation:

- I have the impression that the Devil enjoys passing from one person to another, aggravating the situation of each one. I remember a woman, who was coming to me for exorcisms and was not able to participate in Mass or receive Communion with peace on account of the violent reactions that she experienced. After her deliverance, she went to daily Mass for six months without any difficulty. One day, she went to pray with a charismatic group where, unbeknownst to her, a certain possessed person was also present who manifested during the prayer. Immediately, she began to manifest, and lose control of her self, reacting violently to the prayers. That's when her

Calvary began again and, once again, she was subjected to exorcistic therapy.
What happened?

Did the demon pass over from that man to her? It's possible.

- I make a point of trying to avoid contact between the person I have just seen in my last session and the one awaiting his session. I do this because sometimes when they meet, the person I just finished with returns to the same state he was in moments ago and I have to continue my prayers with him.

  What happened there? Did the demon in the person waiting to be exorcised pass over to the person I just finished with? Not to be dismissed.

- Further, if someone is not suffering spiritual problems of a demonic nature, but it is psychologically fragile, he might fall into autosuggestion, and start manifesting in a way that seems demonic, but, in fact, is not.

- Many people go to these community prayer meetings out of morbid curiosity, cultivating an unhealthy desire for exotic phenomena.

- Finally, we are cannot exclude the possibility that such community prayer meetings can be infiltrated by sorcerers who, having suffered economically because the clients have been dissuaded from going back to them, work against that which the priest directing the assembly, creating all sorts of problems for those possessed and vexed people who are there.

- I have been able to confirm that people who attend these community prayer meetings and have had such reactions, upon attending other churches to pray where there are no demonically afflicted people, no longer experience such reactions.

MY METHODOLOGY TO VERIFY DELIVERANCE[28]

In my daily experience, when I do an exorcism over a person, there is always a deliverance, if only temporary. In other words: unable to bear the exorcism, the devil prefers to leave, if you only for a while. Sometimes, he simulates a departure. I use the following methodology as a verification.

I ask the possessed person to repeat certain invocations along with me. For example," Lord Jesus, I believe in you", "Lord Jesus, I hope and you", "Lord Jesus, I love you", Lord Jesus, bless my husband", "Lord Jesus, bless my children", Lord Jesus, bless my marriage"," Lord Jesus, bless my bedroom."

It happens that, while the person is able to say some of these invocations, others touch the nerve center of the diabolical activity at work on the person. This is a sign that the devil has not left. I have had this confirmed, when repeating the exorcism in its imperative form, he comes back to the surface, reacting furiously. Assurance of the demons departure is only achieved when the possessed person is able to repeat the formula of prayer that touches the nerve center of diabolical activity in his life. When that occurs, the face of the possessed person becomes quite different been during the possession in act.

---

[28] Frair Benigno and I differ on this subject. I do not subsbribe to the theory that a temporary deliverance occurs at the end of each session of exorcism; rather, the demon, like a tired boxer, takes a rest since he cannot endure any more. Although he doesn't manifest, he's present nonetheless.

Even the way in which the possessed person repeats the formula of prayer that I suggest to him, helps me to understand if the demon is still present. When the demon is gone, the words are said with the person's normal voice. When, on the other hand, he is still present, the voice is changed somewhat. The proof is revealed upon repeating the imperative exorcism, and the demon emerges anew.

Even the way one smiles helps me understand if the devil is present or not. If the deliverance has occurred, even though it be a temporary one, a person can smile his normal smile as when he as well. On the other hand, when the smile looks different, it is a sign of the devil still present.

It happens, at times, that the possessed person cannot pronounce the formula of prayer that I suggest him. In order to discover if the demon is still present or not I use this other method. I take the person's hand in mine and divide the prayer, squeezing the person's hand when it's his turn to speak. If he is able to do it, especially mentioning those aspects that touch the nerve center of the diabolical action, it means the devil has left. If, on the other hand, he refuses, it means that the devil is still present: I continue with the imperative exorcism and, then, as a confirmation, I see the devil reemerge, reacting furiously.

CHANNELS THAT SPREAD OCCULTISM

It might be helpful to identify now those channels that spread occultism, that act as open windows for the possibility of extraordinary diabolical activity. I do this so that those who seek the help of exorcists know how to defend themselves from them.

Tattoos and piercings. One of the many channels of diffusion of the occult, esoteric practices, and Satanism into the Western world is presented through tattoos and piercings.

A tattoo is not merely a colored design made on the human body. Nor is it only an image projecting self-expression. There is something more here. Carlo Climati explains it very well:[29] it is a symbol that has its roots in pagan and tribal non-culture of a certain epoch, promoting a non-Christian culture.

It is enough to read the title of the book, *Modern Primitives,* a fundamental text in the culture of tattooism, or its Italian cousin, *Tatuaggi, corpo, spirit,* by Ivo Quartiroli, who concludes his introduction with the hope that "nature be repopulated by plants, animals, and gods" (p. 6).

Which raises the question, which gods does he mean?

The response is to be found between the lines: "we are speaking as well of reappropriation of spirituality, not mediated by moralism or ecclesiastical dogmas. The spirituality that begins with the sensation of being connected. Connected with ourselves, with other living beings, with the earth in the sky. A spirituality that does not need a place of worship, does not need intermediaries, without sin or the sense of guilt" (p. 6).

Thus, concludes Climati in his book, tattoos and piercing are nothing other than "rites of initiation" that make us part of a tribal and primitive cult. They are the new baptism administered by the esoteric non-culture of today. Through bodily modification, Young people adhere, unaware or consciously, to the pagan new age, filled with gods, an empty of the sense of sin.

---

[29] *I giovani e esotrismo. Magia, satanismo e occultismo: l'inganno del fuoco che non bruccia,* ed. Paoline, Milano 2001, pp. 83-91.

The situation seems clear and, therefore more disconcerting, if we glance at the names of the personages who populate Quartiroli's book. Many young people attracted to tattoos have purchased it. And what do we find among the pages of this book?

On page 102 we find a long interview with Anton Le Vey, founder of the American Church of Satan, who expresses his views on tattoos and piercings. In the text, accompanied by a large picture, one finds the address for the Church of Satan. And thus, young people who are passionate about tattoos have the possibility to enter into contact with that satanic sect.

On page 18, young people can find another exponent of the world of occultism, Genesis P. Orridge, follower of Aleister Crowley and foundress of "The Temple ov Psychic Youth". Here too, one is provided with the address of the sect. And so, along with the Church of Satan one can contact the Temple ov Psychic Youth.

It may be added that tattoos often reproduce Satanic and esoteric images that are blasphemous.

Further, magazines that encourage tattoos explain:

> The tattoos that many Polynesian women make around her lips have the purpose of impeding demons entrance into their body through their mouth. The ink itself, with which the design is made, maintains beneficial powers of the god of fire who created it and transmits it to the person tattooed, absorbing it into the skin. The signs are chosen as a way of ingratiating oneself with the gods in order to obtain their benevolence and to placate their ire and its terrible consequences. (*Sacro e profano*, in "Tattoo Gallery", August, 1994).

All of these elements point to what is behind the phenomena of tattoos and piercings. Far beyond fashions considered innocent we find something hidden and disquieting.

Internet. Occultism, writes Climati, finds fertile terrain where there are people in crisis, with difficulties of communication. Loneliness in itself it is already a sign of weakness and vulnerability. And therefore, can provide the entrance of negative messages, bound to the world of occultism.

All of this can happen by way of a computer in the hands of a fragile person who is weak and connected to the Internet.

Many people, above all young people, spend hour upon our before the computer screen navigating the Internet. What types of sites do they find? What messages do they receive?

The passion for occultism, already fed by music in many magazines, finds a privileged point of contact on the net, with dangerous results.

Songs produced by satanic rock represent the first step towards occultism. They can stimulate curiosity for an unknown but fascinating world. With the Internet, people have a possibility to take a further step and their occultist journey. The Internet indeed, can furnish all of the instruments necessary with great ease and speed. One can enter directly into contact with esoteric practitioners, occultists, and Satanists.

It usually begins with the banal search of a term and ends with communication, via email, with true Satanists, offering the person Satanic ritual's righte on their pages that also offer the necessary equipment to do a black mass or a Satanic ritual.

Not long ago, a boy of 13 years used to me for exorcisms. He told me that everything began when, finding himself alone in the house of his 11–year-old friend; she lowered the shades, lit two candles, and began her ritual, which consisted of prayers said in reverse. Most likely she discovered this on the Internet.

A 14-year-old girl told me that while home and connected to the Internet, she got in contact with a satanist who offered her membership in his sect.

Television. Another channel used for diffusion of occultism is television.

It is not uncommon to find programs transmitting messages from sorcerers, witches, astrologists, et al. The most common questions sent to them are:

"Will I find love?"
"How is everything going to workout with my boyfriend?"
"Will I get back together with my ex?"
"Will I find work?"
"Will I pass this exam?"

Certain sorcerers on television have managed to create an air of direct contact with those viewers in crisis. The goal, of course, is to fleece them for as much money as possible after the conversation had on television. How do they do it?

The trick is simple. The sorcerer assumes a serious expression and says something like: "I see important things in these cards, very personal things that I cannot say on television. Come to meet me in my private studio." Or "I can't spend all the time I would like to on the telephone because I have to make space for other callers. If you want to know more come to my studio."

All of this is extremely dangerous. The viewers, in many cases, end up establishing a direct contact with the sorcerer. After the conversation had on television, they meet in the studio and the master-slave relationship ensues. We mustn't forget that we are speaking about people in crisis, psychologically fragile people; people who live in terrible straits and desperation. Consequently, it is not difficult to entrap them in the occult.

Deceit. Another channel used buy occultists is that of deceit. Some occult groups attempt to enjoy the support of the Church in order to present themselves and their work as accredited by it.

Recently I had an encounter with a tarot card reader, she was on the board of the European occultist association, made up of pranotherapists, herbalists, sensitives and tarot card readers. The members of the association obtained tickets to participate in the general audience with Pope John Paul II. The audience took place in the Nervi Hall, and each group had its assigned place. There were some 200 people in the group of occultists. The card reader showed me the document, which granted them participation in the audience, in which the group was identified.

She even showed me a picture of John Paul II as he passed by the group and greeted them, along with various pictures of the group with the bishop who, when being presented by a priest who explained the activity of the occultist association, encouraging them to "continue with their good work of pranotherapists, herbalists, esoterics, and card readers who help heal the suffering of the sick and others." Each one of them was offered certificate with the people blessing. The tarot card reader showed me hers.

And so we find the situation in which a tarot card reader hangs a picture of the pope and a certificate of the papal blessing, a document attesting to the fact that she has been received by the Pope and received his blessing, along with her entire association. How easy to induce people desperate to find a solution for their problems that there is nothing wrong with going to a tarot card reader, asking for help.

The Devil's warriors and mercenaries

This esoteric and occultist bombardment is orchestrated by leaders who know very well what they are doing. They belong to Satanic sect and in their magical doctrine recognize a particular "master". We can call them "the Devil's Warriors". They fight for the devil because they believe in him. Their goal is to spread evil. And, in order to do it, these warriors concentrate, above all, on the corruption of society, focusing on the youth who will be society's leaders tomorrow and will ensure a greater presence of evil in the world.

Aside from the warriors of the Devil, there exist as well mercenaries of the devil. They use occultism esotericism in order to make money. Their goal is not too spread evil, but simply to make money. Horoscopes, magic, séances, and satanic rock music, along with the magazines that published articles about occultism and esotericism, all converge to create a multimillion-dollar industry. And so, as they get rich, they do so at the cost of the others, entrapping them in occultism and esotericism.

The practitioners of magic – write the Tuscan bishops conference in their pastoral note of 1994 – who claim to have powers to resolve problems of love, health, riches, and pretend to take away the so-called "evil eye" and "spells', promote themselves with paid advertisements in the newspapers, showing off their academic degrees and make publicity on the television. It is not an exaggeration to speak of an 'industry of magic' (No. 2).

And so the mercenaries become the warriors' best allies. They play the same game, becoming accomplices in the spreading of evil in society.

CONCLUSION

The 14 stories of deliverance recounted in this book belong to those signs of which Christ speaks that will accompany the faithful. These signs confirm the word acclaimed by his ministers: *These signs will accompany those who believe: in my name they will drive out demons, they will speak new languages. They will pick up serpents (with their hands), and if they drink any deadly thing, it will not harm them. They will lay hands on the sick, and they will recover."* So then the Lord Jesus, after he spoke to them, was *taken up into heaven and took his seat at the right hand of God. But they went forth and preached everywhere, while the Lord worked with them and confirmed the word through accompanying signs* (Mk 16:17).

Such deliverances could simply not be left unmentioned. "Tell of his wonders", the Psalmist enjoins us (Ps 95/6:3). With delight I have accepted that recommendation. That is what brought me to write this book, whose pages narrate the splendor of the glory of God and tell of the wonders of His power, speaking of His greatness. Glory, power, and greatness that have been manifest precisely during exorcisms, bringing the possessed people presented in this book, to their deliverance and healing.

I have seen it with my own eyes and, therefore, feel the need to cry out with great conviction: the mercies of the Lord are without end. And these pages testified to that. Reading the stories we can only conclude that the Lord is truly great, worthy of all our praise for His wonders are without measure.

Prayers against the powers of darkness

Through the sign of the Cross, free from our enemies, or Lord our God.

We flight to your protection, oh holy Mother of God; despise not our petitions in our necessities, but deliver us from all danger, oh glorious and Blessed Virgin.

Comforter of the afflicted, pray for us. Help of Christians, pray for us.

Mary, Mother of Grace, Mother of Mercy, protect us from the enemy, and receive us at of our death.

St. Michael the Archangel, defend us in battle; BR safeguard against the wickedness and snares of the devil. May God review can, we humbly pray: and you, O prince of the heavenly hosts, by the power of God, test down the hell Satan and the other evil spirits, who prowl through the world for the ruin of souls. Amen

Made in the USA
Middletown, DE
24 May 2018